The Purple Martin

NUMBER FIFTY-TWO
THE CORRIE HERRING HOOKS SERIES

The Purple Martin

Robin Doughty and Rob Fergus

UNIVERSITY OF TEXAS PRESS

AUSTIN

Copyright © 2002 by the University of Texas Press
All rights reserved
Printed in Hong Kong

First edition, 2002

Requests for permission to reproduce material from this work
should be sent to Permissions, University of Texas Press,
Box 7819, Austin, TX 78713-7819.

(∞) The paper used in this book meets the minimum requirements of
ANSI/NISO Z39.48-1992 (R1997) (Permanence of Paper).

LIBRARY OF CONGRESS CATALOGING-IN-PUBLICATION DATA

Doughty, Robin W.
The purple martin / Robin Doughty and Rob Fergus.
p.   cm. — (The Corrie Herring Hooks series ; 52)
Includes bibliographical references (p.   ).
ISBN 0-292-71615-X (hardcover : alk. paper)
1. Purple martin. I. Fergus, Rob, 1968– II. Title. III. Series.
QL696.P247 D38 2002
598.8'26—dc21
2001004250

Contents

Figures

Tables

Acknowledgments

Many people interested and engaged in conserving Purple Martins have generously shared information, ideas, and opinions about their favorite birds. We are indebted to all of them.

We acknowledge special assistance from Nature Society personnel, especially Karen E. Martin, editor; the Purple Martin Society (North America), notably executive director Terry Anne Suchma; and the Purple Martin Conservation Association, especially James R. Hill, director.

Individuals have been most kind in making suggestions and comments about the book. We thank Kevin Anderson, Joseph Bell, Mrs. Dan Bromley, Charles Brown, Virginia Carmichael, Tom and Maria Dellinger, Terry Giles, Gay Gomez, Kenneth Hawk, Eric Horvath, Ian Manners, Barbara Parmenter, Carlyle Rogillio, Alexis Wolstein, and Glen Wooddell.

Martin landlords who responded to requests for information and generously shared their knowledge, expertise, and perspectives include Paul and Nancy Albertson, Jim Barden, John Barrow, Dorothy K. Bertany, Tiffany Beyer, Robert Black, Dave Crans, Michael P. Brown, Jim Daly III, Glenn Davis, Linda Davis, Dennis and Linda Fayant, Paul Fodor, Leslie W. Fogleman, Burt Fowler, Tony Frederickson, Raymond Gingerich, Valentine and Evelyn Gohs, Susan and Jerry Gomori, Diane Green, Tim Hammonds, Sheila Hanson, Bobby Harmon, Donald M. Hayes, Dan Heacock, Jeff Hicks, Benny Joe Hite, Allen and Hannah Hudson, Vic R. Jodts, Al Johnston, Kent Justus, Keith Kimmerle, Kenny Kleinpeter, David and Pamela Kunze, Keith and Linda Lawyer, Jim Leedom, Sherri Lewis, Harold Loy, David Mair, Beverly McCullough, Cindy Mead, Tom Mills, Marty Moore, Brian Morris, Terry Ogletree, Earl Parquette, Tharon Paup, Frank Prekup, Ray Revette, Brian Ringham, Don Robertson, Scott and Christina Rumley, Ken Rupkalvis, William Schnoebelen, Jan Siberry, J. Stewart Slack III, Jim Slater, B. Snell, Gary Tessneer, Sarah Thompson, Dave and Teresa Van Booven, W. Wates, Bill Wonchoba, and Rita Woods.

We thank Bill Bishel and Carolyn Wylie at the University of Texas Press for facilitating this project, and June Osborne for commenting on the manuscript. Sins of omission and commission are to be laid at our door.

R.D., R.F.

The Purple Martin

Introduction

*I*t is 6:30 A.M. in late April: a strange assortment of liquid chirps, chortles, and muffled yodels threads the dimness about to be burnished. In a nearby yaupon, a cardinal hammers mellow chinks into the still-black earth. Overhead, Purple Martins lance dawn—expressing their invisible presence through these baubles of sound that hang, as do the minstrels, in the dew-rich air. Some older birds have been around Austin, Texas, for six weeks or more; others are hauling toward them and their dawn song. This chorus will continue as martins chortle for mates and new members for their colonies. Is their voice a sheer fling, an upwell of life at its pinnacle of encounter and renewal, as a poet would opine? Perhaps these birds call in the manner of watery leviathan whales, which also seek kinship and solidarity. For the Purple Martin itches to associate—with others of its kind, with humans who proffer houses and roosts, with additional migrant and resident bug-eating swallows—over great distances. Geography neither restricts nor contains this species. A site will last for eight to twelve weeks; a region is a neighborhood for a season; a migratory corridor is a huge plume of fellows chasing one another for hundreds and hundreds of miles, sliding high and low, stretching wires or bending tree limbs from one season to the next; and a range is where martins begin and end in the Western Hemisphere—scouting the southern reaches of Brazil's lowlands in December and the northern edge of human habitations on Canada's Great Shield in June.

This book is about a special relationship—the regard, affection, and understanding we have increasingly come to express about a bird that responds more and more to our concern for its survival. The Purple Martin is a wild bird that thrives around human habitations and, like other swallows, has responded to land clearance and settlement by adjusting to farms, towns, and even cities. This bird shows an unusual tameness in selecting and occupying compartments or "houses" in which to build its nest and is unique among avians in relying on human-made accommodations in which it nests throughout the core of its range. We treat the martin as both tenant and friend. We guard nest colonies and derive pleasure and satisfaction from watching birds prosper and numbers grow. We find martins companionable, useful, and ebullient. In the United States, they are harbingers of glad tidings—the shift of the season—from winter cold to the life-giving warmth of spring.

Martins pick us out. Increasingly seeking, if we believe old-timers, our hubbub on which they cast their own. It must be the foods that farmers furnish: a suite of insects from crops and fence lines, water from rivers and lakes to slake their thirst and dab on parasites, and, of course, nest gourds and houses. Like Rome's famous geese, they repay us with a wall of sound, startling in its sharp, hard edge for danger; mellow in round dulcet chords, like a troubadour's song of nostalgia and hope—longing for perfection. Under their umbrella I am safe. Cool dawn heralds the sun so that their bustle, like mine, will busy us both. Domesticity is their chore: adventure awaits me when I observe them. I can fly in my imagination, be patient in my cycle, and watch theirs—this year and the next.

Classification: Species and Names

Purple Martins are aerial acrobats. Flinging themselves after insects, these large swallows swoop and glide over towns, pastures, and crops in North and South America. In addition to hawking over farmlands, rivers, and lakes, Purple Martins visit cities, forests, mountains (in the U.S. Great Basin, for example), and sea coasts. These seasonal migrants belong to the swallow family, called Hirundinidae in Latin, and DNA experts place Purple Martins in an even larger family, which includes nuthatches, tree creepers, wrens, titmice, kinglets, bulbuls, and Old World warblers and babblers. Reportedly, Purple Martins diverged from this primitive family about 50 million years ago and from closer swallow relatives some 11.5 million years ago. The genus *Progne* to which the Purple Martin belongs is one of fourteen genera within the swallow family (there is an additional genus of river martins restricted to Africa, which some experts separate into another subfamily). Within this widely spread New World genus, seven martin species are generally recognized with similarly colored plumages, shapes, and behaviors. The Purple Martin is the most well known and admired of these species.

The Purple Martin is one of four North American birds with names describing them as purple. However, mature adult male martins are actually a deep iridescent blue. A length of eight inches and a wingspan of eighteen inches makes it the largest North American swallow, almost the size of its nemesis, the European Starling. The term martin is a proper name in French and derives from the Latin "Mars," the Roman God of War. The diminutive "ten" or "tin" is a pet name, leading to speculation that "little mars" refers to the first month of the yearly calendar—the warring season, when first so-called scouts arrive in the United States.

Martin Species

The Purple Martin is only distantly related to four Old World swallows that are also named martin—Sand Martin (genus *Riparia*), Crag and Rock Martin (genus *Hirundo*), and House Martin (genus *Delichon*). Purple Martins are more closely allied to additional New World relatives—Southern Martin, Gray-breasted Martin, Sinaloa Martin, and Caribbean Martin. These species are so closely related that some experts classify them as one inclusive superspecies. Others argue that these related martins are actually subspecies of the Purple Martin and suggest that a fourth Latin American species, the Brown-chested Martin, is also very similar (see Figure 1). Regardless of taxonomic classification, even experienced birders are hard-pressed to identify female and juvenile martins—all have brown on heads and backs and gray on their underparts.

Male Purple Martins (*Progne subis*) are almost identical with male Southern Martins (*P. elegans*), which nest in south and west South America (including the Galapagos Islands). The male Southern Martin has a similar dark blue body with blacker wings and a longer, more forked tail. It is also slightly larger than the Purple Martin but can be told apart only in the hand. Adult females are duskier brown below with pale edges to their body feathers, making them appear more scaly than female Purple Martins. In general, the female Purple Martin has a pronounced gray forehead and a gray collar around the nape of her neck. Her underparts are also a smudged gray. This gray coloration distinguishes her from similarly colored Latin American martins, which have whiter bellies and contrasting chest and undertail coverts.

Both Southern and Purple Martins may associate together in northern Argentina and in the upper reaches of the Amazon River when Southern Martins migrate north during their winter. Both species flock into towns, villages, and cleared areas, catching insects over rivers and farmlands. An estimated 250,000 Southern Martins roosted in downtown Iquitos, Peru (about 1,600 miles from a major stopover for Purple Martins in Manaus, Brazil), during the late 1970s. A flock of 25 South-

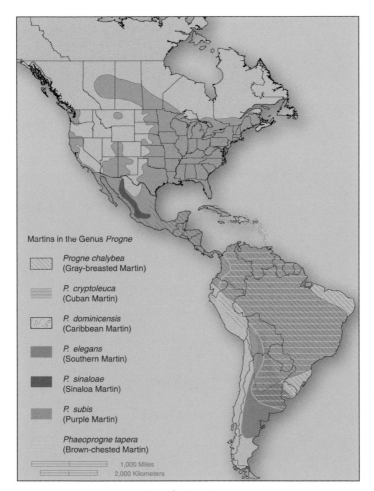

FIGURE I. Purple Martin range map.

ern Martins flew around Leticia, Colombia, in July 1975. This dark species turns up as far north as Panama, and a specimen was taken in Key West, Florida, on 14 August 1890.

The Purple Martin also resembles the Gray-breasted Martin (*P. chalybea*) and Brown-chested Martin (*Phaeoprogne tapera*). Smaller than the Purple Martin, the Gray-breasted Martin is widely dispersed throughout lowland areas of northern South America, nesting from north Argentina (including Mendoza and Buenos Aires) northward to the Yucatan Peninsula and southern Tamaulipas and westward to Nayarit, Mexico. It ranges west of the Andes from northwest Peru. In Costa Rica, the Gray-breasted Martin is locally common to abundant up to about 5,600 feet above sea level, frequenting open areas around buildings where it roosts on wires and bridges.

Experts argue that graybreasts are the most numerous and widespread members of the genus and also are the least sexually dimorphic. Graybreast males have steel blue upperparts but lack the dark blue belly of Purple Martin males. Both sexes have blue on the forehead (not gray as the female Purple Martin) and white undertail coverts. Female and juvenile Gray-breasted Martins are similar to males but are a duller blue above and have less contrasting below. This martin frequents villages and towns, where it nests in roofs and spires, colonizes cleared areas relatively quickly, and can be looked for near water. Texas bird author Kay McCracken noted this species as common in the lowland areas of northern Mexico. Rarely occurring above 4,000 feet, the graybreast seems to seek out human dwellings, stated McCracken, whereas Purple Martins appeared to breed more commonly on the higher Central Plateau. In general, North American records for vagrant martins tend to be for older specimens, as difficulties of field identification make recent records hard to substantiate. Old Texas graybreast specimens are from Rio Grande City, 25 April 1880, and Hidalgo, 18 May 1889.

The Brown-chested Martin, recently placed by some experts in its own genus (*Phaeoprogne*), is restricted to Central America and generally east of the Andes in South America, where it spreads south to north-central Argentina (including Mendoza and Buenos Aires). Sometimes difficult to identify, it is dull brown above and white below, like other female and young martins, except for a distinct gray-brown breast band. Some observers remark that brownchests look like oversized Bank Swallows due to their brown backs, wings, tails, and breast bands, or even like Solitary Sandpipers in flight. This martin reportedly flies closer to the ground than its cousins and seems more sluggish, perching for long periods along riverbanks. It is quite common in open country, nests singly in termite mounds or abandoned *hornero* nests, and mingles with other swallows near open water when not breeding. A much-photographed individual occurred on Cape May, New Jersey, in November 1997, and another was on Monomoy Island, Massachusetts, 12 June 1983.

The Caribbean Martin (*P. dominicensis*) lives in the West Indies (except Cuba). Males have blue on the head, back, and tail, like the male Purple Martin, but show a white lower breast. This color contrast makes male Caribbean Martins relatively easy to identify. Both females and juveniles have gray-brown underparts and may be confused with female graybreasts.

The Caribbean Martin inhabits open country along coasts and reportedly nests in cliff crevices. On Puerto Rico, the local name *golondrina iglesias* suggests that the species also nests in habitations, including churches, and palm trees. This martin breeds from the Virgin Islands to as far south as Tobago, and it winters somewhere in South America.

The Sinaloa Martin (*P. sinaloae*) is a very similar species, formerly considered a race of the Caribbean Martin. It breeds in the pine-oak uplands of western Mexico along the Pacific slope of the Sierra Madre Occidental between 3,500 and 7,500 feet (from central Sonora south to Jalisco). No one has seen this species north of Mexico, though experts speculate that vagrant Sinaloa Martins will eventually be identified in southern Arizona. This bird also probably migrates into South America in the nonbreeding season.

Finally, in the West Indies, there is a Cuban Martin (*P. cryptoleuca,* meaning "hidden white" after the white on the lower belly feathers of adult males), which is restricted to Cuba and the Isle of Pines. It has been recorded in Guatemala and three times in Florida—Key Biscayne on 19 May 1858 and undated specimens from Clearwater and Key West. Apart from these white belly feathers, the Cuban Martin looks like the Purple Martin and nests in cities, towns, and in snags on salt flats, such as on the Zapata Peninsula. Nobody is sure where it passes the winter months after it leaves Cuba.

Migration and Range

The Purple Martin migrates between North and South America (southward from August to mid-October; northward from late January to April) via the Gulf of Mexico and the Caribbean coast of Central America. The species breeds in southern Canada, the United States, and northern Mexico and, in the nonbreeding season, forages mainly east of the Andes in northern South America (for example, Colombia), south into Bolivia and southeast Brazil. In the mid-1980s, the Brazilian Association for the Preservation of Wildlife estimated that 6 million birds wintered in a two hundred–mile section of São Paulo State.

On migration: in Costa Rica, for example, observers note that flocks of Purple Martins appear to fly higher than other swallow species and keep more to themselves, although experts believe that some Purple Martins mingle with resident Gray-breasted Martins. In Panama researchers note that martins mix with other swallows as they migrate along the Caribbean shore. There are only sporadic reports, usually in fall, of Purple Martins along the Pacific coast of Central America.

With a latitudinal span of 85 degrees (from about 35° S to at least 50° N latitude) or 5,600 miles, the Purple Martin is one of the most widely distributed and most easily distinguished birds in the Americas. Purple Martins have crossed the Atlantic Ocean successfully on several occasions (although current lists of rare birds do not include them). As far back as 1840, a bird was shot near Kingstown, Dublin, Ireland. There are three old records from England. In 1842 two specimens were taken over Kingsbury Reservoir, Middlesex, near London, and twelve years later a single Purple Martin was shot at Colne Bridge, near Huddersfield, Yorkshire, about two hundred miles north of London.

In North America, the Purple Martin is a common breeding bird throughout the South, with so-called scouts arriving in south Texas and other Gulf states from about the third week of January onward. It nests in highest densities from central

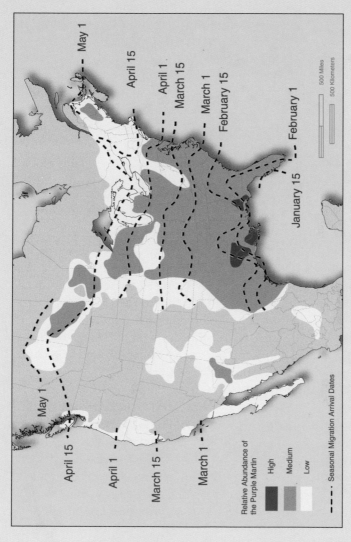

Relative Abundance of
the Purple Martin

High

Medium

Low

--- Seasonal Migration Arrival Dates

500 Miles
500 Kilometers

May 1

April 15

April 1

March 15

March 1

February 15

February 1

January 15

May 1

April 15

April 1

March 15

March 1

FIGURE 2. Purple Martin breeding range map.

and south Texas (generally east of the 102° W meridian) through Louisiana, central Mississippi, Alabama, Florida, central Georgia, South Carolina, and coastal North Carolina (see Figure 2). Breeding Bird Surveys identify highest densities in the parishes of Plaquemines and Jefferson in Louisiana and in Henderson County, east Texas. Nesting martins spread more thinly up the Atlantic Seaboard as far as southern New Jersey and southern Pennsylvania.

From a breeding nucleus in south Louisiana, notably around New Orleans, Purple Martins nest commonly up the Mississippi River Valley, the Ohio River Valley, and reach into Wisconsin and Minnesota. The species is scarcer around the Great Lakes and in New England, though a pocket of birds nests in Maine and spills into New Brunswick, Canada. Elsewhere in Canada, the Purple Martin is most commonly encountered in Manitoba (to about the 52° N latitude) and Saskatchewan, although nesting occurs around Edmonton and Calgary, Alberta. There are reports of martins breeding five hundred miles north of the United States–Canada border, west of Lesser Slave Lake. In British Columbia, martins breed in boxes around Vancouver, Nanaimo, and Victoria.

While the nominate form of the Purple Martin occurs as far west as the mountains of New Mexico and Arizona's Chiricahuas, an outlying population of Purple Martins belonging to a smaller, paler race, *P. s. hesperia,* summers in the desert country of southern Arizona. In 1889 William Brewster named this race but was unable to distinguish *hesperia* from *subis* males, although female western martins have generally whiter underparts and a more whitish collar and forehead than female Purple Martins in the east.

Progne subis hesperia birds arrive in late April and select nest cavities in saguaro cacti in south-central Arizona west to the Ajo Mountains and north to Pinal County. In this arid country, as elsewhere, birds fly from nests well before dawn and search for insects high in the sky. Curiously, in spring, Arizona's desert martins arrive after the martins that inhabit colder basin and range country farther north; however, some desert birds remain until October before heading south into Mexico.

Bridget J. Stutchbury has studied these saguaro-nesting birds. Though at most, two or three pairs of western martins select woodpecker holes in each large cactus, birds interact as a colony with those in adjacent cacti and use valley cottonwoods when not near their nests. One noteworthy Purple Martin roost (consisting of both *hesperia* and *progne* subspecies) existed in Tucson from 1909 through 1947. At that time, the Purple Martin was a common sight over the Arizona city.

A small population of the Pacific race of the Purple Martin (*P. s. arboricola*) nests in the Rocky Mountains, northern California, and western Oregon, with colonies extending into Puget Sound in Washington state and northward into British Columbia, Canada. Very similar in color with *P. s. hesperia,* and slightly larger than the birds in the east, this subspecies nests in Colorado's Rocky Mountains, selecting snags and old woodpecker holes in burned areas.

Authors suggest that this mountain-dwelling subspecies may have special habitat requirements. The Pacific race of the Purple Martin breeds around lakes and in forests generally above 5,000 feet above sea level. Purple Martins are rare in the Rocky Mountains (including Idaho and Utah) and the Pacific West and have recently disappeared as a breeding species in the Chiricahua Mountains in southeast Arizona.

A century ago, western Purple Martins were more abundant and efforts are under way to increase numbers by setting up houses. In 1998 Eric Horvath conducted a survey in Oregon, tallying slightly more than seven hundred pairs, mostly in single-cavity wooden boxes or gourds. From merely half a dozen pairs in the 1980s, numbers in British Columbia climbed to about 150 pairs in the late 1990s, and experts reckon that nest boxes are helping. They encourage landlords to set out more martin houses. Interestingly, famous biologist, author, and environmentalist Aldo Leopold set up a martin house in Albuquerque, New Mexico, in 1918, speculating that "this bird may not yet have become domesticated in the west." He asked for information about nest box use, having discovered martin nests in pine snags in Lake Mary and Coleman Lake, Coconino County, Arizona. Leopold appears to have failed to attract these favorites.

FIGURE 3. Western Purple Martins are much more dispersed than conspecifics east of the Rockies and frequent solitary nest boxes and old woodpecker holes, like these in Oregon. Photo courtesy of Nature Society, Purple Martin Junction, Griggsville, Illinois. Nature Society is the original Purple Martin organization, est. 1962.

FIGURE 4. Western martin house east of Portland, Oregon, along the Columbia River, set by David Fouts in the mid-1980s. Photo courtesy of Nature Society, Purple Martin Junction, Griggsville, Illinois. Nature Society is the original Purple Martin organization, est. 1962.

Colonial Regard:
Early Interest in Martins

*E*arly American settlers admired the Purple Martin, especially handsomely plumaged males colored a deep iridescent blue. Rather than avoid villages and farms, the bold and useful swallow-like bird preferred to nest in and around homes and outbuildings like the swallows and martins in Europe.

John Banister noted how Native Americans "hang Gourds on the top of poles, in which build small birds, of the swallow or Martin kind." The purpose, Banister reported in his *Natural History of Virginia, 1678–1692*, was to harass crows and keep these and similar pilferers away from corn plots and barnyard fowl.

In 1709 John Lawson included the Purple Martin on his list of American birds. He described two kinds—one resembled the House Martin in England (the Eurasian swift, Barn Swallow, and Northern Wren also had equivalents in America, he claimed), while the second was "as big as a Black-Bird" (referring to the Blackbird *Turdus merula,* a common species in England). Planters "put Gourds on standing Poles" for this "warlike" martin, which chased crows, as Banister had noted. Early commentators admired these feisty birds, believing them useful and attractive.

Fellow Englishman Mark Catesby included a painting of "a dark shining" male Purple Martin (see Figure 5) in his *Natural History of Carolina, Florida, and the Bahama Islands (1731– 47),* noting that "they breed like pigeons in lockers prepared for them against the houses, and gourds hung on poles for them to build in." Like Lawson, Catesby reported martins as feisty because they drove off crows, hawks, and other poultry-stealing vermin.

One of the earliest observers to actually study Purple Martins was the Mexican priest José Antonio Alzate Ramírez (1729– 1799). The Purple Martin was one of three swallow species that Alzate closely observed in his attempts to discover the truth about the seasonal disappearance of what are now known to be migratory birds. As a corresponding member of the Académie des Sciences de Paris, Alzate debated the theory of bird migration with such notables as Georges Louis Leclerc, Comte de Buffon (1707–1788). In arguing against those who believed that birds migrate to "flee the cold of winter, in order to find insects in abundance," Alzate noted that martins arrive in the town of Ozumba, forty-two miles north of Mexico City, in February, when it is still cold, and depart in June, when insects in Nueva España are "too abundant and the weather is very hot." Alzate even placed small metal bands on the legs of these birds, proving, in one of the first recorded instances of bird banding, that individual birds return to the same nest sites each year.

Early in the 1800s, famous painter John James Audubon described the martin's life history in five pages of his *Ornithological Biography* (vol. 1, 1831). Audubon admired this bird as a "privileged pilgrim, and the harbinger of spring," which demonstrated courage in mobbing predatory birds, solicitude for its mate, pugnacity in facing danger, tenacity in defense of its nest site, and an admirable confidence around human guardians. This bird artist reported "a general practice" in Louisiana of putting up nest houses for the Purple Martin. In "almost every country tavern" and "all our cities," residents set up boxes, he explained, even youths who killed wild birds seldom disturbed these public favorites. In the United States two hundred years ago, people recognized and welcomed the Purple Martin and adopted a custom that had predated European colonization.

Audubon and others noted that Native Americans (specifically Choctaws and Chickasaws) admired "watchdog" martins and hung nest gourds from cut saplings or cross branches near their encampments. According to Audubon, these sharp-eyed swallows mobbed vultures, which grabbed dried meat and deerskins. African Americans in the South also preferred the bold cheery species—symbol of freedom, he insisted—by attaching a gourd "to the flexible top of a cane" near their dwellings.

FIGURE 5. Mark Catesby's early rendition of the Purple Martin.
From *Catesby's Birds of Colonial America* by Alan Feduccia.
Copyright © 1985 by the University of North Carolina Press.
Used by permission of the publisher.

Affection for the Purple Martin among European and Afro-American farmers appears to have increased throughout the 1800s. In March 1862, according to authors Louise and Ann Chambers, bored and homesick farm boys of the 42nd Ohio Regiment built and nailed up martin houses from so-called cracker boxes—wooden crates, each of which held a day's supply of hardtack for fifty men. The regiment was laying a successful siege to New Madrid, Missouri, from an encampment along a swampy section of the Mississippi River. The wood boxes they tacked to cottonwoods and posts attracted a "huge population of martins," and, thenceforth, these Civil War troops were known affectionately as the Martin Box Regiment.

En route to Florida at the close of the 1800s, artist and ornithologist Bradford Torrey observed martins around calabashes hung from tall poles in rural areas of the South. "I had noted these dangling long-necked squashes everywhere," he penned, "and had wondered what they were for." He got his answer from a local man near Tallahassee, who told him that "there's no danger of hawks carrying off the chickens as long as the martins are round." Torrey was pleased to see how the gourds were "the colored man's martin-boxes."

Torrey represented a growing cadre of early twentieth-century writer-scientists committed to instructing teachers and children how to identify and study wild birds. People interested in outdoor natural history judged the Purple Martin a friend of humanity, in what famous birdman and Audubon's contemporary, Alexander Wilson, termed "half-domestication." Companionship was an endearing trait. Martins flocked to nest boxes set up near human residences, whose inhabitants admired the comings and goings of their bird guests during spring and summer. People swapped tales and tidbits of gossip about martin behavior. This practice of observing birds at close quarters, monitoring arrivals, how young grew and fledged, and in what month they all flew away caused many Americans to regard the Purple Martin as "*the* 'bird-box' species of this country."

With such friendliness, accessibility, and boldness, observers used the Purple Martin to answer general puzzles about birds, including migration. For example, one warm drizzly day in February 1821, Audubon observed a large martin flock "about a mile in length, by a quarter of a mile in breadth" spiraling over New Orleans. As the martins swept northwest, he resolved any confusion about whether they fell into a torpor during colder months or hibernated underwater in lakes (speculations current at the time). Audubon knew he was seeing a massive migration. The martin's "powers of flight, which even violent winds failed to conquer," he declared, was steering birds north; after nesting, such swift-winged migrants left early, especially from southern states (by 20 August), Audubon noted. Such effortless flights and speedy migrations caused the birdman to argue, presciently as it turns out, that the Purple Martin "must go farther [into South America] . . . than any other of our migratory landbirds."

Audubon's contemporary and authorial colleague, Scottish immigrant Alexander Wilson, also speculated about the movements of Purple Martins (he reported them as far north as Hudson Bay, Canada) as contradicting the so-called doctrine of torpidity. According to people who supported the idea of hibernation, martin disappearances in August spelled a nap— for up to eight months under water and ice—Wilson noted incredulously. He also correctly opined that birds set out for a more congenial clime "on the first decline of summer" and didn't hibernate.

Homes for Martins

Someone has built a purple martin house
far up a pole, in the foreground to the left,
a house like ours in miniature with ten ways into it,
or out, so we can guess what staying home would mean.

Kathleen Peirce, "Practicing Joy," from *Mercy*
(Pittsburgh: University of Pittsburgh Press, 1991)

Wilson, like Audubon and other experts, loved the martin's dash and zest manifested by flight, calls, and song. Such humanlike vigor inspired admiration. Wilson mentioned John Joseph Henry, Supreme Court Justice of Pennsylvania, who, in 1800, employed a carpenter to erect apartments on his farm near Harrisburg only to have bluebirds contest martins for space. The judge believed that the lively predawn warbles from martin houses, which he eventually filled with the correct species, woke up drowsy laborers. As another enthusiast put it a generation later, "as the industrious farmer hears the pleasing call to labor, and associates with this favorite bird the idea of an economical, cheerful, and useful guest."

Wilson reported how martins took possession of a box in the garden of the famous naturalist and plant collector John Bartram and roosted in local dovecotes, crevices in houses and stores, and so forth, on a regular basis. The bird's bravura led Wilson to declare, "I never met with more than one man (a close-fisted German) who disliked the Martins, and would not permit them to settle about his house."

Nest sites for martins included gourds, simple cigar boxes, miniature mansions, plus apertures and awnings in all kinds of buildings, including the columns of the U.S. Patent Office and Post Office in the nation's capital during the 1870s. Humanly supplied sites could be as high as a flagpole capped by a large ball, into which martins entered through a crack, which loomed 130 feet above Seattle, Washington, and as low as a palmetto piling about three feet above Anna Maria Key, Florida.

It is a steadfast species, declared early admirers, declining to change its nest site like the returning robin. Nor was it fickle about whether to use a nest box, like the bluebird, nor as casual and untidy as the wren. The Purple Martin, according to T. H. Whitney, who pioneered and promoted martin houses in Atlantic, Iowa, used the same box year after year, provided it was weather proof and sturdy. Whitney believed that the birds selected the same chambers, thereby demonstrating a marvelous combination of navigation and memory from one season to the next.

One hundred and fifty years ago, the martin's predilection for carpentered dwellings set on poles in gardens and yards was a common and widespread trait in the United States, except in the West, where Thomas Nuttall, writing about Oregon before 1850, noted that Purple Martins selected "knot-holes of the oaks." There, he reported, Purple Martins "did not appear to court the society of man." Recognition that these scattered populations of martins, which summer in the Mountain West, Pacific coast, and saguaro desert of Arizona, prefer woodpecker holes in limbs and snags rather than bird boxes remains a subject of commentary.

Martins and Bird Protection

This is a lonesome place without those birds, just like if your family left you and moved out of the house.

George Finney, owner-builder of a
620-room martin house, Winnfield, Louisiana

*T*he Purple Martin figured in the origins of bird protection in the United States, specifically in the establishment of the Audubon Society. In founding "The Audubon Society for the Protection of Birds," in the sportsman's weekly *Forest and Stream* (11 February 1886), George Bird Grinnell, naturalist, hunter, and expert on the American West, noted an alarming destruction of native birds. Hunters shot a wide variety of species, including "bright-plumaged songbirds," as well as sea- and waterbirds, including ducks, geese, and other game species, for meat, skins, and feathers. Owner and editor of the weekly journal, Grinnell reported that in February 1886, one New York dealer had sold 200,000 bird skins as millinery and that London outlets auctioned more than 750,000 birds for fashionable feathers in a three-month period. A New York establishment "recently had a contract to supply 400,000 skins of American birds to one Paris firm," complained Grinnell, who recognized that scores of beautiful and useful species fell to the guns, traps, and snares of millinery agents.

The galloping destruction of the nation's avians, according to Grinnell and other colleagues, was inhumane, scientifically reckless, and jeopardized the "balance of nature," which insectivorous birds, like swallows and martins, helped maintain. In his two-column entry about bird protection in *Forest and Stream*, Grinnell explained why an Audubon Society, a so-called antiplumage league, was needed. He referred to Otto Widmann's study of a Purple Martin colony near St. Louis, Missouri, to clarify and justify his position.

By monitoring sixteen pairs of martins, bird lover Widmann calculated that one set of parents made 312 daily visits to a nest box, delivering "not far from 2,000 agricultural insects" to growing young. People should stop killing these and other beneficial species, declared Grinnell, and seek to enforce existing bird laws, pressuring legislators to expand protection for nongame birds, such as martins.

Based in Park Row, New York, Grinnell's new Audubon Society issued the *Audubon Magazine,* "to create a rational interest in birds." The journal underscored the economic value of wild animals. A three-page article titled "The Purple Martin," appeared in July 1887 and reinforced claims about the martin as a "useful" bird that chased "hurtful insects" around homes and guarded poultry. Neither quarrelsome nor harmful, martin colonies "dwell together in the utmost harmony" assured the author incorrectly. Each community member "is just a sturdy, hardworking citizen of the bird world, who is determined to stand up for what he considers his own rights, and who is afraid of nothing that flies," the author concluded.

This freedom-loving native species (albeit a summer visitor), exemplified the virtues of American citizenship, family life, thrift, industry, energy, and personal initiative. Reportedly, the martin brooked, incorrectly as it turned out, no nonsense from usurpers, such as increasingly entrenched populations of foreign sparrows. Cheerfully voiced, brilliantly colored, graceful in shape and flight, the Purple Martin was touted as a favorite among Audubon members, who joined the new society in droves until Grinnell decided to suspend the publication and disband the organization. He was simply overburdened by the expense and time needed to run the Audubon Society to which 48,862 people had subscribed by 1889.

Grinnell's bird protection society drew attention to the murder of native birds for millinery and meat markets. The Audubon Society (which revived on the state level in the mid-1890s and grew into a national association in 1902) steered a back-to-nature impulse that identified and studied, not killed, native species. Schoolteachers interested their pupils in the lives of birds as a way of learning about the outdoors and finding in nature lessons about human morality and the virtues of citizenship.

A "birds as little people" approach in the early 1900s included common species like the Purple Martin, which related to humans better than many native birds, accepted gifts of nest homes gladly and without complaint, and were easy to observe. They were not finicky about the quality of human-made domiciles, and often proved fairly tame. Bird expert and custodian of the Public Museum, Milwaukee, Wisconsin, Henry Nehrling summarized their good qualities by insisting that martins are "as well satisfied with the simple hollow gourd attached to a pole . . . as with the most ornamental and best arranged Martin-house." By living close to their human benefactors, martins appeared grateful and companionable.

In the shift from shooting birds to studying them in field and garden, enthusiasts worked hard to "earn their keep" as they jotted down the gamut of martin antics, chuckled birdman and famous nature writer John Burroughs. Burroughs wrote about Purple Martins because people recognized them and admired their behavior. Rather than nature lovers seeking out wild birds, hinted bird writer Neltje Blanchan, wild martins seemed to seek out nature lovers. Blanchan published books about birds and bird-watching for urban Americans and included the Purple Martin among a list of the "birds that live near us." Classified as "conspicuously black" in one of ten color groups, Blanchan's Purple Martin was welcome in a picturesque, rustic suburban setting. "Set on a pole over which honeysuckle and roses climbed from a bed where China pinks, phlox, sweet williams, and hollyhocks tumbled, martin houses always seemed to have a pair or two of these large, beautiful swallows circling overhead," noted Blanchan. Garden America—secure, beautiful, and tranquil at the end of the city trolley line—included decorative, showy (and useful) Purple Martins. Distinctly New World in their size, brilliance, and assertiveness, the martins were, however, under increasing threat. Blanchan knew that House Sparrows usurped the boxes of her "pampered darlings of luxury" because the intruders refused to nest in natural cavities.

Avian Competitors

In 1897, when she was writing *Bird Neighbors,* Blanchan had not hardened her heart about the competitive proclivities of starlings (though she clearly disliked House Sparrows), excusing the starling's reputation for driving native birds away as being "by no means as black as he has been painted." Within a decade or so, most outdoor writers reported that "hoodlum" sparrows and equally hoodlum starlings were wreaking havoc among martins and other favorite birds.

Competition between martins and the introduced House or so-called English Sparrow, and European Starling, for nesting space exacerbated tensions within the ranks of Audubonists and bird sympathizers. Enthusiasm for these feisty foreigners, especially House Sparrows, which successfully first bred in Green-Wood Cemetery, Brooklyn, New York, where enthusiasts released them in the early 1850s, turned to dismay. The success of granivorous sparrows, shipped from England largely to deal with caterpillars that defoliated trees in city streets and parks, reinforced, polarized, and prolonged opinions about good and bad birds that early twentieth-century educators hoped to soften.

Universal judgments about the sparrow being a "bad" bird (some termed it a winged rat) were due to its success in the United States. Alien sparrows also failed to check bugs; one noted ornithologist claimed that one pair of Purple Martins will destroy more insects in a single season than all the sparrows in a township will consume in a lifetime, and sparrows usurped the nest spaces of indigenous birds, including the martin. The pugnacity of the House Sparrow, amplified in the 1880s by another misfit, the European Starling, alarmed bird lovers, especially as martins and sparrows began to fight over favorite nest houses. The failure of martins to cope with tenacious sparrows continues to dog nest providers, who advise one another how to control the pesky foreigners.

Initially, some authors, such as Widmann and Burroughs, held a grudging respect for the House Sparrow due to its toughness but soon realized that as martins flew off to hunt "this is the time when the Sparrows sneak into the boxes" to destroy martin eggs. After he attempted to broker a compromise by building homes for both sparrows and martins, Widmann (whom Nehrling cited admiringly) decided that "the Martin is too much dependent on the weather to be a successful defender of its home" and commenced (in 1888) to destroy sparrow nests "without mercy, by any means, and at every time of the year."

Humans have continued to take sides in the "war" between the alien sparrows and starlings and the native martins, and suggestions about how Purple Martins best vanquish these bullying Europeans have multiplied. Organizations dedicated to martin welfare conclude that sparrows and martins cannot coexist. Efforts to promote a truce ended with one major association in 1984, when the Nature Society, Griggsville, Illinois, reported that martin nests suffered widespread destruction from usurper sparrows. Suppression and eradication of alien House Sparrows in martin colonies is a common topic of both e-mail chat room conversation and correspondence in current periodicals. Sparrow traps are easily attached to aluminum martin houses.

First issues of *Bird-Lore,* an Audubon Society periodical owned and edited by American Museum ornithologist Frank Chapman, dedicated pages to the protection of birds, including the Purple Martin. In 1912 "The Story of Peter, a Purple Martin," recounted how an injured young bird proved alert, tame, companionable, and spirited after Fanny Eckstrom began to feed it houseflies (150 per day). Peter began to tease Fanny's pet dog and cat and exercised its wings regularly, until her brother released him outdoors and she "never saw him afterward." This charming children's tale evokes compassion and concern for birds as "little people" who deserve our admiration for their strength of character in being like humans and who yet retain a sense of mystery We hope that Peter flew off to join companions as they headed south for the winter.

The rhythm of bird migration, seemingly transcendent to earthbound human activities, affected bird scientists not given to emotion. Experts P. A. Taverner and R. H. Swales investigated bird migration over Point Pelee, Ontario, Canada, in

August 1907. After passing a hellish mosquito-bitten night on the shores of the peninsula that remains a crossing point of bird migrants over Lake Ontario, they awoke to observe the first movements of a martin or two overhead about half an hour after sunrise. As the light increased, single martins became a stream, which flowed as "a succession of impassionate birds, all hastening under a mysterious impulse . . . converge on this little spit of sand." It was a usual migration of a common species, they admitted, but it touched them deeply. These hard-bitten birders, who shot specimens as they passed, realized that they were witnessing the migration as "a never-ending procession passing from one unknown to another." The flight of martins struck them as dignified and determined. Birds flew at all levels in a steady, deliberate, and unhurried movement in the sky "as inevitably as fate," declared the ornithologists, who exulted in being witness to still-mysterious wild birds.

The Purple Martin achieved a more elevated form of social, rather than biological, gravity in March 1908, when it appeared on the list of ninety-two birds that President Theodore Roosevelt found on the White House grounds or the larger area of the capital during his administration. The president of the United States recognized and admired a friendly bird citizen, and so did hordes of school-aged children who began to more carefully study the lives of such common species.

However, not everyone welcomed Purple Martins. While more and more people built or purchased nest boxes, others grew frustrated by huge flocks that circled roost sites (sometimes with swallows or grackles) in late summer. Some roosts favored by martins have drawn commentary and grown into tourist venues. In August 1905, T. Gilbert Pearson, an active and prominent executive in the fledgling Audubon movement for South Carolina, came upon a frightful slaughter of ten to twelve thousand Purple Martins in Wrightsville Beach, North Carolina. Local residents had objected to noise and dirt from an estimated 100,000 martins, which congregated each evening in a grove near the small community.

One dusk, a group of local men armed with shotguns walked under the birds and began firing into massed ranks. Every volley killed or maimed hundreds. Pearson, who was pushing for enforceable laws in the Carolinas at the time, learned of this slaughter and helped prosecute twelve men, who received nominal fines for killing an officially protected species. The incident showed how cavalier some people were toward wild birds; however, the killing generated widespread publicity and helped turn sympathies toward the Purple Martin and other insectivores.

Economic Ornithology

The question of usefulness has dogged the Purple Martin. Popular and promotional utterances champion the bird's taste for mosquitoes and other noxious insects. Indeed, one reason for erecting martin houses is to rid properties of biting insects and horticultural pests. When biologists from the U.S. Bureau of Biological Survey's Division of Economic Ornithology examined the stomach contents of martins, experts grew less certain about the heralded merits of the Purple Martin. Clarence Weed, entomology professor, and Ned Dearborn, assistant curator of birds in the Field Museum, Chicago, published a manual of economic ornithology in which they called the martin "a great insect eater." Unfortunately, however, the species did not discriminate between injurious and beneficial insects. Apiarists charged hungry martins with snatching honeybees. Dragonflies, predators of other pest insects, also turned up regularly in diets of nestling martins. Weed and Dearborn admitted that "young birds certainly make a poor showing for the usefulness of the species"; however, they discovered that adults fed on nefarious squash beetles, locusts, and tiger beetles.

An exhaustive 1918 study discovered that merely five of two hundred stomachs held honeybees (all of them drones) and that martins ate mostly ants and wasps. Pesky houseflies, horse flies, boll weevils, and cucumber beetles also entered the plus column for martins. In the early 1940s, Arthur Cleveland Bent, who drew from ten publications about the bird's food habits, noted that most investigators "are entirely commendatory of the martin's economic value." However, Bent praised the species as a useful insectivore, while admitting that one or two investigators had found it "rather neutral" in regard to being valuable for farmers and horticulturists.

Literature and Society

Poets and nature writers discover in avians symbols and suggestions about humanity. Often, birds mirror life's intensity through their full-throated songs and varied behaviors. They master such a wide range of environments in all seasons, exemplifying many skills necessary for survival. People have long noted these traits and have drawn from various species lessons about human society—such as deciding to plant crops after noting the passage of cranes, for example, or observing that many species appear to mate for life and tenaciously defend mate, territory, and offspring.

Curiously, scant attention appears paid to the Purple Martin in American letters. Emerson admired the chickadee, Tennyson the owl and swallow, Flagg the bobolink, Thaxter the sandpiper, and Burroughs the Eastern Bluebird. However, T. S. Eliot regarded the martin as "the dancing arrow" among a dozen species he included in a 1963 poem "Cape Ann."

Carl Sandburg (1878–1967) called martins "slingers and gliders" in a 1920 poem "Purple Martins" in his collection entitled *Smoke and Steel*. He contrasts their aerial acrobatics with the stolid earthbound tread of humans:

Twirl on, you and your satin blue.
Be water birds, be air birds.
Be these purple tumblers you are.

Dip and get away
From loops into slip-knots,
Write your own ciphers and figure eights.
It is your wooded island here in Lincoln park.
Everybody knows this belongs to you.

Five fat geese
Eat grass on a sod bank
And never count your slinging ciphers,
your sliding figure eights,

A man on a green paint iron bench,
Slouches his feet and sniffs in a book,
And looks at you and your loops and slip-knots,
And looks at you and your sheaths of satin blue,
And slouches again and sniffs in the book,
And mumbles: It is an idle and a doctrinaire exploit.
Go on tumbling half over in the water mirrors.
Go on tumbling half over at the horse heads of the sun.
　Be water birds, be air birds.
　Be those purple tumblers you are.

The Purple Martin appears, as a casual reference or together with other animals, another dozen or so times in nineteenth- and twentieth-century poetry. Like Sandburg, many authors refer to its agility in the air; others admire its vitality. Yusef Komunyakaa contrasts death ("hangman . . . drops the black hood" over the condemned man) with the live martin swooping past with a jade-green dragonfly in its bill. In "The Palms" (1993), author Charlie Smith includes the martin in a passage about a lonesome traveler who meanders across the country in an old car, staying in cheap motels, isolated and wounded by his father's abuse of his mother. The martin is a catalyst "nudging yourself toward more life," not despair. Such literary allusions draw attention to the bird's verve, industry, and dash—features commonly admired by landlords who watch over their colonies. The martin is a presence, a shard of energy with its "holiday life."

Life History Studies

Most of what we know about martins comes from the careful observations of either martin landlords or university-trained

FIGURE 6. Premigratory martins gather on wires prior to departing for South America in the fall. Courtesy John L. Tveten.

scientists. Though many early bird people admired the Purple Martin, Widmann was the first observer in the United States to make systematic observations of the species near St. Louis, Missouri, in 1884. Thereafter, ornithologists made little more than passing references to martins in the established ornithological journals until Joseph Jacobs published two accounts about his growing colony in Waynesburg, Pennsylvania, in 1903 and 1909. The first detailed life history study of the Purple Martin began a generation later, when in 1938 Robert W. Allen, a student at the University of Michigan, initiated a daily study of local colonies. Allen's graduate thesis reviewed migration, nest sites, territory and pair bond formation, and included details about the breeding cycle. Unfortunately, Allen was killed in New Guinea during World War II, and the results of his study were published posthumously in 1952.

A decade earlier, Alexander Sprunt Jr. drew from notes and correspondences with other bird-watchers and professional ornithologists to compile a comprehensive account of the Purple Martin to be included in Arthur Cleveland Bent's serial *Life Histories of North American Birds*. This work remains an informative treatment of the martin.

Additional enthusiasts took an interest in martins. J. W. Hardy studied martins at a colony in Murphysboro, Illinois, from 1938 to 1952 and collaborated with R. F. Johnston in monitoring behavior in a colony in Lawrence, Kansas. Observations led the two experts to publish the classic paper on martin visual displays and social interactions in 1962. During that decade, J. L. Wade (1966) and R. B. Layton (1969) authored popular books that increased public awareness and appreciation for Purple Martins. Their volumes and the growing trade in martin houses attracted additional students. In fact, the promotional literature of martin enthusiasts sparked H. W. Hale's 1968 rebuttal of claims that martins routinely eat thousands of mosquitoes.

Research on Purple Martins expanded in the 1970s, when Jerome A. Jackson and J. Tate Jr. studied nest box use by Purple Martins, House Sparrows, and starlings in eastern North America, and S. Rohwer and D. M. Niles pioneered work on the implications of martin subadult plumages and delayed arrival times.

However, during that decade, the most prolific Purple Martin researcher proved to be Charles R. Brown—a teenager who took copious notes of martin behavior in his backyard colony near Dallas, Texas. Brown has published over twenty papers on martin biology, including nesting and fledging activities, and continues to actively research and write articles on martins.

During the 1980s, Eugene S. Morton began publishing observations on martin ecology, breeding behavior, and vocalizations. Rather than mere descriptions of martin activities, his studies regarded the Purple Martin as a "model organism" to test competing theories of evolutionary ecology.

Martin publications increased after the Purple Martin Conservation Association (PMCA) and its magazine, *Purple Martin Update,* was founded in 1987. This organization continues to promote popular and scientific articles about martin life history in order to provide members with the latest information about martin biology and guidance about landlording. It also encourages martin landlords (people who monitor colonies) to record observations carefully so that a fruitful union of professional and amateur research may be sustained and new insights generated.

During the last decade, technological innovations have opened up novel opportunities to study Purple Martins. In 1992 the *Purple Martin Update* published an account of Charles McEwen's videotape of the martin nest cycle from inside a martin compartment, giving enthusiasts their first glimpse of previously unobserved brooding and parenting activity. The rise of comparative molecular studies in biology has also improved our understanding of Purple Martin evolution. F. H. Sheldon and D. W. Winkler's DNA analyses revealed that martins are descended from ancestral Bank Swallows. In the field of migration studies, Kevin R. Russell and Sidney A. Gauthreaux Jr. took advantage of improved NEXRAD radar technology to study large martin roosts in South Carolina. By observing patterns of rings generated by martins leaving their roosts, they were able to document the dynamics of foraging and roosting during the martin's autumnal migration. Purple Martins continue to provide numerous opportunities for interested researchers.

Life of the Purple Martin

They'd rush up in one huge gust,
in a turbulence outside themselves.

David Wojahn, "No Language We Know," from *Icehouse Lights* (New Haven: Yale University Press, 1982)

*E*ach Purple Martin starts off as a fertilized egg inside its mother's oviduct. After a full day of formation, she deposits the egg in the nest, where the embryo develops for fifteen to seventeen days before hatching (see Box 1). The martin hatches by piercing a small egg sack inside the egg, thereby filling its lungs with its first breath of air. The tiny bird then chips out a small line of shell around the middle of the egg. After the martin weakens the two halves of the shell, it struggles into the nest, naked and totally dependent on its parent for warmth. Though helpless, the hatchling begins to orient to its world, recognizing sounds made by the adults. Though its eyes are still developing, a newborn martin probably distinguishes light from dark as day passes into night.

As the baby Purple Martin grows in the nest, it huddles with several siblings, which all hatch within a day or two. Upon hatching, the 2.75–3.5-gram nestling barely lifts its head when the parents bring food. As the youngster grows, however, it gains strength and develops senses of taste and smell. After about ten days, it begins to open its eyes and hone a visual acuity so critical for life on the wing. By the time it is ready to leave the nest, the fledgling will know how food tastes, smells, and looks. It will also recognize and understand the meaning of its parents' call notes, learn martin songs, and have interacted with both adult and fledgling neighbors in and around the nest cavity.

About two weeks after hatching, the young bird moves forward in the compartment and anticipates parent visits. Young martins gape at adults and passing martins in hopes of obtaining

Egg Formation and Embryo Development

THE UNFERTILIZED OVUM that will become a Purple Martin undergoes a phase of rapid development in which the addition of yolk causes the cell to swell in size and burst from the ovary. Within about fifteen minutes, the ovum is fertilized by a sperm cell and passes to the oviduct, where over the course of several hours it receives a layer of egg white or albumen. Albumen is composed of three types of protein: mucin (5 percent), globulin (5 percent), and albumin (90 percent). The egg then passes down the oviduct, where it receives two thin shell membranes. Finally, it enters the uterus, where it is coated with the mostly calcium carbonate shell. The shell is formed with thousands of tiny pores that allow oxygen into the egg, and the exterior of the egg is entirely covered with an extremely thin organic cuticle forming a waterproof protection and bacterial barrier.

Egg formation lasts about twenty-four hours, and the pure white egg weighs about four grams when laid in the nest. Most of this weight consists of the yolk and albumen proteins that will nourish the growing embryo.

When the egg is laid, the martin embryo is a tiny blastoderm or germinal spot on the surface of the ovum. Unlike mammals, the sex of the embryo is determined by the genetic contribution of the mother. Male sperm provide a Z sex chromosome, whereas the unfertilized ovum can contain either a Z or W chromosome from the mother. These chromosomes combine to form a male (ZZ) or female (ZW) embryo.

The ovum and embryonic martin are suspended within the egg by twisted chords of albumen (chalazae) attached to opposite ends of the yolk. When the egg is turned in the nest, the chords allow the ovum and embryo to rotate inside the egg. This keeps the lighter portion of the embryo up and the heavier part down and orients the developing embryo to the earth's gravitation.

After several days, the embryonic martin has developed a heart, and blood vessels extend throughout the egg. Within a week, it will have a head, tail, and rudimentary legs and wings. While its lungs are developing, the embryo receives oxygen through a highly vascularized membrane that connects the gut of the martin to the inner membrane of the shell. This membrane also allows the martin embryo to remove waste from its system in the form of insoluble urate crystals. These inert crystals are deposited harmlessly inside the egg while the embryo develops.

As the embryo grows, it fills the space inside the shell and begins to move with repeated, spastic actions. Over time, the tiny bird will begin to coordinate these actions into smooth and deliberate movements, allowing it to spin inside the egg. Eventually, the martin must assume a position that will allow it to hatch. It tucks its head under its wing, which breaks the inner egg membrane and provides oxygen from the air sack. Breathing with its lungs for the first time, the little bird is ready to break out of its shell.

tasty insects. Young and parents both close their eyes as the food is passed, and if one or the other drops an insect morsel, the nestling will not recognize it, and it will remain in the nest until removed by a parent. Older nestlings usually defecate out of the nest hole, but after receiving a meal, a young martin may swivel and excrete a fecal sack for a parent to carry away. As it grows, the nestling jockeys with siblings for position at the entrance and may even scramble onto the porch of the birdhouse to vie for dragonflies and other insects supplied by attentive parents. Pushing around the nest hole can be dangerous and so can passing food. A martin landlord in Florida observed a young bird accidentally pulled from a nesting gourd by a parent when the nestling mistakenly latched onto the adult's beak during a feeding visit. Others have found dead nestlings with enormous dragonflies sticking out of their mouths—probably choked by items too large for them to swallow. Young birds grow increasingly alert and develop individual temperaments as they interact with one another and their parents.

Martins are most susceptible to predators during the four weeks between hatching and fledging. Any predator that enters or reaches into the nest cavity will kill or remove very small

TABLE 1. *Nest Predators and Competitors*

Predators (most frequent marked with *)	Nest Competitors
Raccoon*	European Starling
Eastern Red Squirrel	House Sparrow
Virginia Opossum	House Wren
Barn Owl	Tree Swallow
Great Horned Owl*	
Barred Owl*	
Eastern Screech-Owl*	
Greater Roadrunner	
Blue Jay	
American Crow	
Fish Crow	
Black-billed Magpie	
Black Rat Snake*	
Yellow Rat Snake*	
Corn Snake*	
Fox Snake*	

TABLE 2. *Purple Martin Ectoparasites*

Martin Bird-nest Mite *Dermanyssus prognephilus*

Nasal Mite

Feather Mite

Blowfly *Protocalliphora splendida*

Lousefly *Hippoboscidae*

Blackfly *Simulium meridionale*

Mosquito *Culicidae*

Bird lice (4 species) *Myrsidea dissimilis, Philopterus domesticus, Machaerilaemus americanus,* and *Bruellia brevipes*

Fleas (2 species) *Ceratophyllus idius* and *Ceratophyllus niger*

Bedbugs (5 species) *Hesperocimex coloradensis, H. sonorensis, H. cochimiensis, Cimexopsis nyctualus,* and *Ornithocoris pallidus*

nestlings (see Table 1). Many landlords lose nests and even entire colonies to marauders. Snakes and owls are perhaps the most common intruders, though one landlord in Georgia was startled to find fire ants swarming into his gourds and attacking the nestlings. From about two weeks old, young birds begin to fear intruders and to huddle against a far wall whenever danger threatens. In addition to ground predators that include raccoons, skunks, and squirrels, competitors for nest boxes such as House Wrens, House Sparrows, and European Starlings frequently peck at eggs and nestlings; a score or so of external parasites also afflict young birds (see Table 2).

Nest parasites feed on skin and body fluids and may weaken a nestling beyond its ability to recover. Though martins have coevolved with such parasites, James R. Hill III has noted that martins in his Pennsylvania colony fledged almost twice as many young after he removed ectoparasites—suggesting that body parasites may be responsible for nestling mortality at rates in some cases approaching 50 percent. It is not known how widespread this problem is across the martin's breeding range.

As they mature, older nestlings stretch and beat their wings inside the nest compartment and, during the final days before fledging, perch and flutter on available porches. When a young martin leaves the nest, it follows a parent, often early in the morning. Its first flight is unsteady—the inexperienced bird beats its wings rapidly, flares its tail, and moves anywhere from a few feet to several hundred feet before grabbing a branch, wire, or snag. Experienced fledglings fly for five to ten minutes without difficulty, but first-timers may even require nudging from parents to stay airborne.

Older birds in the colony, especially second-year (SY) birds, often harass fledglings as parents lead them away from the colony with frequent choo calls. Over the subsequent week, fledglings become accomplished fliers. Speculation about why older birds harass fledglings has centered on their supposed intent to discourage juveniles from imprinting on the natal colony, thereby reducing future competition for nest space; or perhaps more plausibly, to prevent fledged young from returning to the colony and taking food from nestlings. Recently fledged birds can easily return to nest compartments and snag food carried in by adults by perching on porches or nest entrances.

In a study of a dozen martin colonies in Maryland and Virginia, Eugene Morton and Robert Patterson discovered that adults did not appear to distinguish between their own young and intruders (hence the advice to human landlords to place any downed fledgling in a nest with similar-aged young). This so-called kleptoparasitism of food may be lessened when adults, often first-time breeding SY birds, chase and mob the unnerved fledglings because they also have unfledged young in the colony. The SY birds tend to nest later and so their young are likely to suffer if older, fledged birds steal food intended for still-growing progeny.

A brood of four or six birds may take up to three days to fledge, during which time the parents will gather their free-flying progeny in an area close to but usually out of sight of the nest colony. A Texas study showed that this assembly area was within a mile or two of their colony. After all young have fledged, the parents will escort them farther afield. At a wastewater treatment plant in Austin, Texas, a new colony of martins (in 2000) led their young to a fence line bordered by eight-to-ten-foot-high bushes and fed them some three hundred yards from the nest gourds. Several dozen young birds congregated on the exposed snags and remained in the area for several days before dispersing.

For the first two days after fledging, a young martin takes food from a parent, which perches at its side. On the third day, the individual learns to grab food dropped by a hovering adult. On the fourth day, it begins to fly out to greet incoming parents and receives food transfers in the air. Observers have noted that some parents recapture insects bungled by juveniles. This training evidently teaches young birds how to find and capture the prey species they learned to recognize in the nest. After four days, juveniles begin catching food for themselves and probably become fully independent three or four days after that.

Martins feed on many flying insects and readily consume other arthropods that become airborne, such as spiders (see Table 3). Despite claims, there is no evidence that martins eat mosquitoes in large quantities; studies reveal that mosquitoes comprise no more than 3 percent of a bird's average diet. Purple Martins seize prey in midair by locating insects visually. Foraging birds dive up or down and sweep from side to side in order to capture their food, presumably locating prey against a backdrop of both earth and sky. Like most swallows, Purple Martins have eyes on the sides of their heads—giving them at least a 220° field of view, so that an individual may locate an insect flying alongside it with one eye, then turn to view it with both before seizing it. Like most songbirds, martins can probably see into the ultraviolet light spectrum, giving them superior color vision that aids them in spotting insects.

While hunting, martins often alternately flap and soar in wide circles, often at heights of 150 or more feet above the ground, though they may sweep for insects lower down in cold weather. Martins fly at speeds of 5–40 mph, averaging about 20 mph while hunting over open areas, often near rivers and lakes They are efficient hunters and usually spend less than 50 percent of their time searching for food. Rain and temperatures lower than about 48° F inhibit their ability to find insects.

Throughout the week or so that juveniles are under parental supervision, the young birds make repeated exploratory forays throughout their natal area. Adults lead their progeny to sources

Nestling Development

DAY 1   The bird is tiny, pink, naked, and weighs about 2.75 grams. Its eyes are closed, and it cannot hold up its head for more than a brief feeding. The hatchling dangles its wings and legs at its side and uses them for support when begging for food. The bird rests on its belly with neck curled and head tucked in the same general position it assumed in the egg. Birds may gain up to 4 grams in the first day.

DAY 2   The bird has more than doubled its hatching weight.

DAY 3   It averages 10 grams.

DAY 6   Dark gray patches of feather tracts begin to develop on the wings, head, and back, and eyes begin to open a little more each day. Small sheathed feather tips (pinfeathers) appear on the wings. The young bird is beginning to hold its head in a resting position and can right itself if turned on its back. Birds approximate 20 grams in weight.

DAY 7   Pinfeathers sprout from the wings.

DAY 8   Pinfeathers appear on the tail, giving a youngster a mostly gray color. Its average weight is 30 grams.

DAY 10   The eyes are fully open, and the pinfeathers are breaking to expose the tips of the flight feathers. Fluffy down feathers begin to cover the body. A bird averages 40 grams in weight.

DAY 12   Most of the body is covered with gray down. Nestlings orient toward the nest entrance.

DAY 13   The young bird averages 50 grams and may turn to defecate from the nest hole.

DAY 14   Emerging feather tips extend more than an inch beyond their sheaths, and pinfeathers are still visible on the back. Birds huddle at the back of the nest compartment in response to parental alarm calls or when faced with an intruder.

DAY 15   The white feathers on the upper-middle back are conspicuous.

DAY 16   Feathers continue to emerge from their sheaths.

DAY 17   The nestling begins to wait for its parents at the nest entrance. Most of the feathers are out of their sheaths, and dust from breaking sheaths shows as white powder on each bird's back. In the next few days, the individual will reach its maximum weight of 60 grams.

DAY 20   Birds usually have begun preening.

DAY 21   Wing feathers extend to the base of the tail.

DAY 22   Birds begin to lose weight, and some may successfully fledge at this age.

DAY 24   Wings cover the white feathers on upper-middle back.

DAY 26   Wing feathers extend along the body to the middle of the tail.

DAY 28   Wing feathers extend to the tip of the tail or beyond. The average weight is 50 grams, and most nestlings will fledge on or before this day.

TABLE 3. *Martin Foods*

Coleoptera
  Scarabaeidae   scarab beetles
  Curculionidae   snout beetles
  Carabidae   ground beetles
  Cerambycidae   long-horned beetles
  Euphoridae   flower beetles
  Rynhophora   snout beetles
  Cincadelidae   tiger beetles
  Nitidulidae   sap beetles

Hemiptera
  Corimelaenidae   Negro bugs
  Pentatomidae   stink bugs
  Membracidae   treehoppers
  Coreidae   leaf-footed bugs
  Lygaeidae   seed bugs

Diptera
  Tipulidaae   crane flies
  Chironomidae   midges
  Muscidae   muscid flies
  Asilidae   robber flies
  Culicidae   mosquitoes
  Syrphidae   syrphid flies

Odonata
  Aeshnidae   darners
  Libellulidae   common skimmers
  Coenagrionidae   narrow-winged damselflies

Homoptera
  Aphididae   aphids
  Pentatomidae   stink bugs
  Membracidae   treehoppers
  Cicadidae   cicadas

Hymenoptera
  Ichneumonidae   ichneumon wasps
  Siricidae   horntails
  Formicidae   ants
  Apidae   bees
  Chalcidoidea   chalcid wasps

Lepidoptera
  Nymphalidae   brush-footed butterflies
  Danaidae   monarch butterflies
  Lasiocampidae   tent caterpillars

TABLE 3 *continued*

Orthoptera	
Acrididae	short-horned grasshoppers
Tettigoniidae	katydids
Trichoptera	caddisflies
Isoptera	termites
Ephemeroptera	mayflies
Araneida	spiders

of water and to grit for digestion, as well as to best locations for food. Families may return to their nest compartments at night and during cold or stormy weather. Once the juveniles are independent, however, young birds are more likely to roost away from the colony. Individuals probably separate from siblings soon after becoming independent but continue to use martin houses, passing nights in compartments of more distant colonies. How far juveniles range during their first summer is undetermined, though observers have recorded birds as far as nineteen miles from their fledging site. Although they stop roosting in their birth colony, juveniles frequently return there, especially during early morning. Some young birds fly back to their birth colonies six or seven weeks after becoming independent and even claim or defend cavities by lunging at passing individuals.

As the summer progresses, young Purple Martins begin to join older birds in traditional premigratory staging areas, where hundreds or thousands of individuals roost for several weeks before starting migration. Roost sites are scattered across North America (see Figure 7) and include stands of trees, wires, towers, buildings, and bridges. A recent web page about martin roosts turned up fifty-nine known sites and an additional twenty-six suggested by radar imagery in the United States. Most of them are in the South, with Texas and Louisiana leading with fourteen and ten sites, respectively. However, there is a marked bias toward the Mississippi and Ohio River Valleys, suggesting that many Purple Martins key into these and other river systems as they move across the United States. Not surprisingly, only one site is known in the Pacific Northwest—in Portland, Oregon, with less than sixty birds; and only one is in

the High Plains, in North Dakota. Most roosts are east of 100°
W longitude.

Traditional roost sites may be used for several years, or even
decades, before martins abandon them, and larger ones attract
tens of thousands of birds and hundreds of bird-watchers. In
August 1903, P. A. Taverner observed a flock of these peculiar
"haunters of civilization" milling around the Field-Columbian
Museum in Chicago's Jackson Park. They flew west, and colleagues directed him to their nightly roost at the far end of the
Midway in an unlikely spot in three trees on the southeast cor-
ner of Washington Park. Martins landed amid the clatter of
cable cars, lights, vehicles, and "gypsy fortune tellers with their
array of gasoline jacks and the usual quota of loafers." Taverner was impressed by the "agitated, boiling mass" of birds
that gradually settled. As he crept closer and looked up, Taverner remarked that "every branchlet and twig had its burden
of little fluffy feather balls, each with its head tucked between
the joint of its ample wings, and covered with the spread of
shining scapular feathers."

Today, one of the most spectacular sites, one most accessible
for humans, is located on the south end of the Causeway Bridge
across Lake Pontchartrain in Metairie, New Orleans, where observers—such as Carlyle Rogillio, noted for his work on martin
rehabilitation—have estimated numbers in excess of 200,000 in
fall migration. Martins arrive at the urban site as early as late
January, and stragglers roost there into mid-November; highest
concentrations occur from mid-June through mid-July.

Rogillio, who lives near Lake Pontchartrain, knew little about
martin roosts until he observed birds streaming over his house
every afternoon on an easterly heading. He assumed that their
roost was many miles beyond the built-up southern edge of
the lake. By chance, however, he observed the same birds from
a friend's house a few miles away. This time the martins were
headed west, suggesting that their roost was much closer than
Rogillio had thought. He rerouted his jogging path to follow
them and discovered massed ranks of martins over the Causeway Bridge. As they dived toward the water at dusk and disappeared, he assumed they had made off to some distant spot.

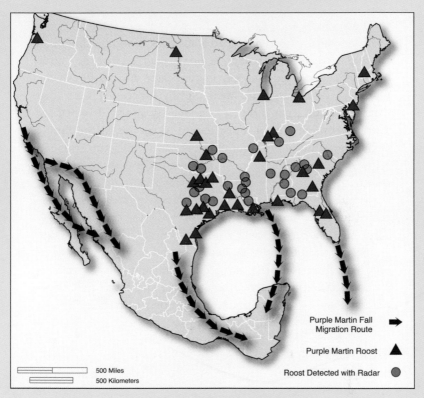

FIGURE 7. Purple Martin roost sites map.

The following year, Rogillio searched for Purple Martins again, and after pushing through scrub and briars along the shoreline, keeping a sharp eye for snakes, he finally realized that the Purple Martins had selected humanly made beams and trestles of the Causeway Bridge itself for their nightly hideout. He recalled that, as the sun went down, a huge martin swarm dropped toward the bridge "like a funnel cloud in reverse as the funnel pulled the cloud of birds out of the sky and under the bridge in just a few minutes." Birds dashed into a tight space between speeding vehicles above and lapping water below.

Stunned by these memories, Rogillio sought to protect this and other roost sites. In 1983 he formed Project Swallow (incorporated under National Wildbird Refuge in 1992) to draw public attention to the causeway roost and protect it. The nonprofit organization dedicated itself to raising over $7 million for a sanctuary, and through his efforts and those of his colleagues, the roost site received the appropriate designation from the Louisiana state legislature in 1990.

Currently, as many as three thousand visitors assemble in an observation area at dusk to witness the rush of martins under the causeway. Over the years, the organization enlisted support from causeway management to set up wire fencing above the guardrails in order to help martins from hitting traffic. Before fencing went up, Rogillio figured that autos and trucks killed as many as twelve thousand birds every year. Migratory individuals and juveniles unfamiliar with the need to keep low as they swung toward the trestles suffered heaviest casualties, he noted. Today, more than a mile of fencing protects martins in this and another roost site toward the north end of the same causeway. Rogillio and coworkers have consulted with transportation officials elsewhere, including Lake Livingston, Texas, about the benefits of fences on bridges where other martins roost.

An hour or so before sunset, birds circle over the causeway's south terminus. Numbers gradually increase until as light fades they gather together, swoop down, and burst in successive "waves" that wash under the causeway from the west. At each pass, more and more chattering martins drop onto beams and other structures until as night settles the few latecomers skid under the causeway and join their companions. The racket from perched birds and the swirl of hundreds together going back and forth almost at water level is most impressive. It seems inevitable that individuals will crash into the lake, but somehow amid all the din and movement, they navigate to a safe landing.

The number of martins in the Lake Pontchartrain roost pales in comparison with another on a small island in Lake Murray, South Carolina. Clemson University biologists Kevin Russell and Sidney Gauthreaux Jr. estimated that at least 700,000 martins used that safe retreat in late summer. These bird experts have also located many additional roosts. In 1996 they joined David Mizrahi in using WSR 88D (NEXRAD) Doppler radar to locate thirty-three large martin roosts in the U.S. Southeast.

Radar studies show movements of martins in and around roost sites. Experts have discovered, for example, that a predawn exodus takes place about ten minutes before sunrise. During the day, birds scatter and forage as far as sixty miles from their dormitory, then head back and begin to circle for two hours or so before settling at sunset.

How martins navigate toward roost sites and nest colonies is open to debate, and researchers do not fully understand how young birds find their way to nonbreeding areas. However, like their cousin swallows, the species has excellent powers of flight and orientation. After being purposefully displaced, for example, individual martins have returned to nest colonies from as much as 150 miles away. Much remains to be learned about martin navigation (and bird orientation in general); however, experts argue that martins use the position of the sun and the earth's magnetic field for pinpointing their position. Foraging flights are presumably made by compass orientation, rather than solely by local landmarks, although a bird may rely on both. Martins are extremely competent way finders, recognizing a nest compartment by its height and orientation. However, tests show that they do not recognize a cavity if a careless landlord switches the house to a new direction while nesting birds are away.

Martins do not migrate in large flocks but set out in small, distinct groups, which travel from one roost site to another along their path north and south. Groups of several hundred birds may spend most of the day together at favorable locations and perch in trees or wires near open areas after feeding. Probably, they migrate at low altitudes during daylight in order to feed as they travel. Large martin roosts along the Gulf Coast in the southern United States (the Lake Pontchartrain site, for example) and along the Mississippi River Valley suggest that many martins from eastern North America fly across the Gulf of Mexico. Others hug the shoreline and pass in large numbers along the east coast of Central America. Birds from Arizona and the Pacific Northwest apparently migrate south along the west coast of Mexico.

Southbound individuals make a lengthy journey lasting three months or more, and birds from scattered geographical areas in North America migrate at different times. Southern birds depart before others that nest farther north. Bird enthusiast Krista Morgan recorded southbound martins passing through Punta Allen, a fishing village in Mexico's Yucatan Peninsula, about seventy miles south of the Island of Cozumel (itself a Mayan name for the Purple Martin) as soon as early July. The martins roosted in pines and on a tall tower, she reported, building up numbers throughout the month until birds "actually darkened the sky" as they circled the site.

According to Morgan's informants, individual martins did not tarry around the roost but joined a general exodus toward Belize, reaching Panama the following month. Large numbers of Purple Martins also pass along the Gulf Coast lowlands of Mexico throughout August, appear in central Colombia at month's end, and migrate into northeast Peru during the first part of September. Though birds have been found in Manaus, a favorite roost spot on the equatorial Amazon River, as early as 2 August, most Purple Martins probably do not reach Brazil until September. During November most birds leave the Amazon basin and head into traditional wintering grounds in southern Brazil.

Very few, mostly unofficial, records exist of martins that winter (and survive) in North America. *Nature Society News* editor Tom Coulson's headline "Martin Family Winters in Kansas" (June 1987) excerpted correspondence from a landlord in Atchison (about forty miles northwest of Kansas City) that de-

FIGURE 8. Some of the seventy thousand martins roosting in January 1985 in the plaza of San José do Rio Preto, northwest of São Paulo State, Brazil, where spray paint tagged thousands of birds. Courtesy of Nature Society, Purple Martin Junction, Griggsville, Illinois.

scribed how two adults and three young stayed on in early December 1986. By feeding on the ground in a nearby pasture on and off throughout the day and roosting together in a cavity of their nest house, the martin family reportedly survived the fairly mild winter. An additional six birds joined the martin group in April 1987.

The landlord, who was used to controlling pesky sparrows and starlings, declared, "I sure worried about them all winter." She remembers that the Purple Martins nested as usual in the two houses she managed that summer. Then, in the fall, she lowered the houses, cleaned them out, and decided to end the dozen-or-so years of landlording.

Other reports of wintering birds come from Orlando (1915) and Tampa (mid-1970s), and there was one report of eleven martins among Tree Swallows near New Orleans in December 1956. It appears that some individuals may survive cold weather in most southerly areas, although bird life histories specialist Arthur Cleveland Bent, writing in the 1930s, judged that even stragglers in Florida "leave the country entirely."

Most youngsters pass their first Northern Hemisphere winter in the sunny climes of southern Brazil. They hunt over gently rolling country planted in sugarcane, corn, and coffee and assemble at dusk in town squares in the Brazilian state of São Paulo. During their stay, the birds enjoy an austral summer with daytime temperatures above 100° F. On the nights of 21–23 January 1985, members of the Brazilian Association for the Preservation of Wildlife, with assistance from the military, sprayed five flocks of roosting martins in five cities in the state of São Paulo with different paint pigments visible under ultraviolet light. Over the following six months, thirty-one individuals of the approximately 200,000 marked birds were identified in eight of the United States and three Canadian provinces (see Table 4). The Brazilian roost of Barretos (fifty thousand birds), in which an orange paint had been used, supplied most recoveries and housed individuals from locations widely scattered across the martin's breeding range in North America.

The first bird recovered was found dead in her nest colony in Duncanville, Texas, forty-seven days after being sprayed at

TABLE 4. *Band Recoveries from São Paulo, Brazil, 1985*

Date	Status	Location	Roost
9 March	dead	Duncanville, Tex.	Barretos
7 April	live	Duncanville, Tex.	Barretos
11 April	dead	Glasgow, Mo.	Barretos
4 May	live	Duncanville, Tex.	Barretos
4 May	live	Shreveport, La.	Barretos
10 May	dead	Ozawkie, Kans.	Ribeirão Preto
12 May	dead	Conway, Mo.	Rio Claro
14 May	dead	Leavenworth, Kans.	Barretos
17 May	dead	Denton, Tex.	Barretos
30 May	dead	Duncanville, Tex.	Araraquara
?	dead	Vincentown, N.J.	Barretos
?	dead	Patuxent, Md.	Barretos
12 June	dead	Fort Erie, Ontario	Barretos
19/20 June	live	Marysville, Pa.	Barretos
19/20 June	live	Marysville, Pa.	Barretos
19/20 June	live	Marysville, Pa.	Araraquara
21 June	live	Laurel, Md.	Rio Preto
28 June	live	Saxis, Va.	Barretos
28 June	live	Saxis, Va.	Araraquara
28 June	live	Saxis, Va.	Ribeirão Preto
29 June	live	Saxis, Va.	Barretos
30 June	live	Saxis, Va.	Barretos
1 July	live	Round Bay, Md.	Barretos
2 July	live	Arnold, Md.	Barretos
?	dead	Spearman, Tex.	Barretos
?	dead	Appleton, Wisc.	Barretos
?	dead	Middlebourne, W.V.	Araraquara
?	dead	Metairie, La.	Barretos
?	dead	Smithfield, Va.	Barretos
?	dead	Stettler, Alta.	Araraquara
?	dead	Oxford, N.S.	Barretos

NOTE: Thirty-one birds identified from about 1,500 live and dead birds examined.

SOURCE: *Nature Society News,* 1985–1986.

Barretos. This adult female, banded in 1982, had made the flight of at least four thousand miles in forty-seven days, averaging eighty-five miles per day. Duncanville bander, Thomas Dellinger, discovered the second martin, a live bird, from the Barretos roost, on 7 April. Thereafter, reports filtered to personnel in the U.S. Fish and Wildlife Research Center in Patuxent, Maryland, who collated reports about live birds and examined wings from dead birds supplied by colony managers. A Barretos martin even turned up in the Research Center's own colony in May. A total of twenty-two Purple Martins sprayed in Barretos were identified in colonies from central Alberta east to Nova Scotia, and clockwise from Chesapeake Bay through New Orleans, Dallas, Kansas City, and into Wisconsin.

Merely 21 of 1,149 martins recovered over more than seventy years of banding have been reported south of the United States. Ten individuals have come from Brazil (seven in the Amazon River valley), three each from Colombia and Bolivia, one from Venezuela, three from Central America, and one from Mexico. Compilers James Hill and Thomas Dellinger suggest that records show that at least some western birds pass southward along the Pacific coast of Mexico and that a cluster of recoveries in Bolivia were from martins banded in the U.S. Midwest, possibly suggesting that birds that nest in the same general area may winter together. The small number of band recoveries makes it impossible to draw conclusions. One Duncanville, Texas, bird (number 4, see Figure 9) averaged 42 miles per day on a 2,950-mile journey to Colombia; another from Alberta, Canada (number 5, see Figure 9), made 53 miles per day before recovery in El Salvador. Another martin (number 6, see Figure 9), banded in August 1975, was recovered in December 1976 in southeast Brazil—some 6,700 miles away from its banding site in Oregon.

By February most adults head north. A delayed molt on the nonbreeding grounds, however, delays the migration of SY birds by several weeks. All individuals stage at various sites along the migratory track, including one large roost in a petrochemical complex in Manaus, Brazil, where many martins remain through

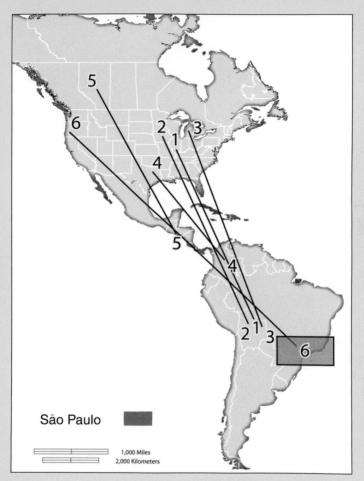

FIGURE 9. Notable Purple Martin band recoveries map.

March (see Figure 10). Purple Martins hug the Caribbean and Gulf Coasts of Central America, though an unknown percentage of them cross the Gulf of Mexico from Mexico's Yucatan Peninsula. Birds swing into Florida by island hopping across the Caribbean or by coming in from the Yucatan via Cuba.

Yearlings usually arrive at nest colonies six weeks or more later than older birds (see Figure 2), but they do not usually return to the colony in which they hatched. Presumably, they head to the same region and perhaps explore colonies they visited the previous summer during their postfledging excursions. Second-year adults are usually the ones that select new martin houses, as older birds return to their previous colonies where they seek to monopolize and defend the best nest compartments. By the time that second-year birds arrive, older males have claimed nesting cavities, and their mates may have begun laying eggs. Newcomers are attracted to established colonies by the dawn song of older males—a lengthy advertising song uttered in the air above the colony. Yearling males seek out sites in established colonies where they court females that prefer the company of other martins.

In choosing a new colony, martins look for houses placed on poles 9–15 feet above the ground in open areas free of nearby bushes or brushy ground cover, some 40 feet or so from taller trees, and about 30–120 feet from a human residence. Martins also prefer sites near open areas, in which they feed, and usually locate within two miles of a freshwater source. They will occupy six-by-six-inch compartments but prefer larger ones if available, especially longer cavities with an entrance hole located a little above the floor. Martin expert Charles R. Brown has demonstrated that martins enjoy greater reproductive success in these deeper nest spaces.

Less-experienced SY birds often have difficulty raising their first brood. Females may construct inadequate and incomplete nests and may lay fewer eggs than older counterparts. Some SY females lay eggs in other SY nests, and older males may cuckold yearling counterparts as they copulate with untended yearling females. It is surmised that some SY females paired with yearling males may seek out older experienced males. Calculations suggest that 70 to 80 percent of the young in a nest guarded by an SY male may not be his own offspring.

Second-year males prospect several colonies in the region before they settle. Oldest males may or may not choose to defend vacant nesting cavities from newly arriving martins, perhaps so that they can attempt to mate with the younger females. Each SY male has slightly different plumage characteristics that allow similar males to recognize one another as they establish and defend new nest sites. Yearling birds that do not manage to establish a nest during their first breeding season become floaters or hangers on in established colonies and often harass young martins as they fledge. Yearling males can even become a threat to other martins. One martin landlord in central Texas has observed these unmated birds raiding nests in his colony and pulling nestlings out of compartments.

Second-year birds are fully adept at communicating by voice and body posture. They sing like older birds and use and respond to the communicative functions of each call (see Table 5). They actively monitor and communicate with each other at the colony, and observers believe that individual birds recognize one another by voice, as fledglings do their parents. There is some evidence that birds must learn at least some of their song from conspecifics: in the absence of other martins, one captive male delivered an amalgam of notes from two other bird species.

After their breeding season, martins begin a complete molt. They join other martins on roosts occupied the previous year and presumably follow the same migratory path to Brazil. The following spring, these individuals returning to North America as third-year (TY) birds arrive at colonies after the oldest birds have already returned and claimed nesting compartments but before the arrival of the second-year birds. Before these yearlings come in, the second-breeding-season males lay claim to nest compartments and vie with older birds. If the bird nested unsuccessfully, it may look for another colony.

If an adult male Purple Martin survives to breed, molt, and repeat the annual migration for two years, it will leave the wintering grounds and arrive in its breeding colony even earlier

FIGURE 10. Migratory stopovers include physical and human-made features. Martins crowd trees; others pass nights in safe, well-lit industrial complexes, such as in this petrochemical refinery in Manaus, on Brazil's Amazon River. Photo courtesy of Nature Society, Purple Martin Junction, Griggsville, Illinois. Nature Society is the original Purple Martin organization, est. 1962.

TABLE 5. *Martin Vocalizations*

Vocalization	Description	Context	Message
Juvenile Call	Single, short, harsh (2–4 kHz), often given 2–3 times/second; given by young birds in nest and shortly after fledging	Solicitation of food from parents	Signals food request
Choo call	Soft *choo* sound (1.5–5 kHz)	Used by flying adult females in leading recently fledged broods	Attracts attention of young
Cher call	Short *cher* sound, given singly or doubly (1.5–5 kHz)	Commonly used in wide range of social situations	May serve to signal identity of individuals
Chortle Call	Short, low multi-note chortle (1–3+ kHz)	Often used before Croak or Chortle Songs —usually while sitting in or near nest site	Signals more excitement than Cher Call
Zwrack Call	Harsh, short *zwrack* note (1–8+ kHz)	Given by adults at end of dive as bird comes closest to intruder, often of another species—only given while diving at intruder near active nest site	Signals high intensity alarm
Zweet Call	Short, one-syllable *zweet* sound (2–4.5 kHz)	Primary alarm call given by adults in presence of intruding predator or competitor	Signals presence of intruder
Hee-Hee Call	Series of 4–10 harsh *bee bee* notes (1.5–4 kHz)	Used by males during intense territorial fighting—usually in or near the nest site	Signals extreme excitement and aggressive intent
Croak Song	1–3 seconds of low croaking (1–3 kHz) and higher grating (1–6 kHz) notes	Male gives in presence of female while attempting to attract a mate	Mate solicitation
Chortle Song	1–3 seconds of chortle call notes interspersed with harmonic down-slurred notes (1–4 kHz)	Given by females, usually towards mate —usually in or near nest site	Possibly signals excitement by female
Subsong	Softer, shorter croak songs lacking grating notes and incorporating initial *cher* notes	Modified Croak Song given by males in various situations late in nesting cycle and during premigratory roosting—usually given in or near nest site	
Dawn Song	Lengthy series of various notes lasting several minutes	Given by males in flight high above colony before sunrise	Thought to attract other martins to nest site in order to enhance colony formation

for its third nesting season. These oldest "purple" males appear at sites several weeks before birds returning for their second season and a full six weeks or two months before the SY birds. They joust for highest nesting cavities that are more secure from pole-climbing raccoons, rat snakes, and such, and will defend several nesting compartments around their favorite cavity.

Adult males defend a site by singing while perched on the ledge of their compartment or close by. The individual defends his territory from other males by adopting a horizontal pose, raising its nape feathers, flicking wings and tail, and snapping his bill. If the intruder persists, the defending male may give chase and fight in midair by facing a rival and locking claws, even tumbling to the ground while uttering a series of four to ten high-pitched *hee hee* calls.

When females arrive, males advertise their nest sites by repeatedly going in and out of cavities and singing to a possible mate while facing out of their nest holes. They also sing in circular flights that begin and end at the nest entrance. The female martin selects a nest compartment and begins to defend it with her mate. Pairs form bonds by roosting and preening together and by singing to each other.

Both males and females build the nest from twigs, grass stems, leaves, and mud. The female usually builds most of the nest, but her mate often accompanies her to prevent other males from interfering. Before the female lays her eggs, both birds usually line the nest bowl with fresh, green leaves. Copulation usually occurs inside the nest cavity. Fertilized eggs are laid in the morning, one per day, until she has completed and begins to incubate her clutch. Older females usually lay five to seven eggs, while younger birds average three or four eggs.

Male birds may be inside the nest compartment during egg laying, and the female usually rests for several hours after laying an egg. She then covers her eggs with more green leaves before leaving the nest compartment to forage. During this time, females lose their lower breast and belly feathers—forming a brood patch of bare skin that they use to incubate the eggs. They incubate sporadically before the clutch is complete;

however, by the time the penultimate egg is laid, the female is spending much time on the nest. The male stops guard duties after his mate starts to incubate the eggs, though he may spend time inside the cavity. He also may cover the eggs while his mate forages, though the male does not have a brood patch. During daylight, females usually incubate three-quarters of the time depending on the weather.

During the two weeks that females sit on their eggs, older males mate with younger females. One male in the colony will often dominate this activity and sire as many as 85 percent of all illicit nestlings.

Within a few hours after hatching, nestlings are fed by their parents with tiny, compact balls of small insects that they form in their mouths while feeding. Parents remove the fecal sacks excreted by nestlings and may cover their young with leaves when away from the nest site. For the first week or so, males and females may alternate feeding the nestlings, with one parent departing on a foraging flight as the other arrives with its bolus of food. However, males often make fewer feeding visits than females. As the youngsters grow, their parents deliver larger insects, especially dragonflies, moths, and grasshoppers (which in rare instances can become lodged in the nestling's throat).

Though the nest season is a busy time for parents, a martin's day is not entirely taken up with parental duties. Adults may pass lengthy periods perched in the colony, preening, or even engaging in "playful" activities. One landlord in Round Rock, Texas, noticed a female come out from her nest compartment with a dead leaf in her beak. After sitting on the porch for some time, she finally dropped the leaf. Before it could hit the ground, she swooped down and plucked it out of the air. The bemused observer watched her fly across the street, drop the leaf two more times and catch it before it hit the ground.

After adults have reared young to independence, they often return to the colony for several weeks and may renew nesting activities, though Purple Martins rarely produce a second clutch and even more rarely manage to fledge two broods. In many years (1976–1999) of keeping track of a large colony in southwest Tennessee, landlord Victor Stoll recorded merely seven second nest attempts among 1,377 pairs that he managed in five of his twenty-four seasons. His statistics show that only .5 percent of pairs attempt to nest again and that a second occurs only once every five years in his colony. Thus, as the summer winds down, adult Purple Martins visit the colony less and less, until they abandon it and join migratory roosts.

Predators, stormy weather, body parasites, and disease take a toll on Purple Martins. Experienced birds may live six or seven years: one in Texas lived for thirteen years and nine months. Only one-third of fledged martins, however, survive their first year. But once an individual lives through one annual cycle, its chance for a longer life improves. Only 2–3 percent of breeding adults die during the nest season, although as many as 40 percent of adults perish each year. This 60 percent annual survival rate for mature birds is double the average survival rate for juveniles.

Prolonged rain, heavy snow, freezing or low temperatures, tornadoes, hurricanes, and drought kill more martins than all other mortality factors combined. Thomas Nuttall and his early colleagues recognized that prolonged bouts of cold or rain limited martin survival by shutting off insect foods. He recalled in coastal Massachusetts, "a few years ago," that many martins died inside their houses during midsummer rains and that "they have since been far less numerous." Commentators have consistently reported die-offs attributed to weather, especially on the edge of the bird's range in New England and Canada.

In 1907 a remarkable spring flight along Point Pelee halted abruptly as cold, wet weather caused "immense numbers" of Purple Martins to line walls, floors, and perches inside sheds and barns. A decade later, another cold spell lasting from the end of April through mid-May decimated martins in the U.S. Midwest. Bird lovers removed dead adults from nest compartments. Research has shown inclement weather is hard on martins. When martins first arrive in the United States, late winter storms or days of unusually cold and wet weather reduce flying insects so that new arrivals may starve. Many huddle together in compartments to conserve body heat and may succumb there.

Landlord of the Year Ed Donath established a way of feeding martins during bouts of cold and wet weather in the 1990s. Using that premise, Ken Kostka of the PMCA worked with an Amish martin enthusiast during a patch of foul weather in April 2000 to throw commercially purchased crickets into the air and observe birds catch and consume them. Since a martin survives four or five days without much food but then soon dies, Kostka explains that tossing crickets as high in the air as possible close to perched birds can get them through. Crickets resemble natural grasshoppers, he says, and after half a dozen are tossed in the air, individual martins begin to dart after them. Other birds copy such behavior. He recalled that when the martins spotted the cricket container the day after feeding they grew excited, captured the first cricket tossed to them, and followed "Andy [Troyer] around . . . looking for handouts like a bunch of seagulls at the beach!"

Hurricanes often flood areas with intense wind and rain that prevent martins from feeding, as happened in 1972, when Hurricane Agnes blasted through the eastern states, killing adults and young along the Atlantic Seaboard, Pennsylvania, and elsewhere. In August 1945, winds in excess of 120 mph over Matagorda Bay, Texas, grounded and injured "thousands of martins" going south. Bad weather wipes out both local and regional populations—as happened in New England in 1903 and again in June 1929, when heavy rain caused adults and young in eastern Massachusetts to starve. Wet springs also take a toll of birds. In 1966 monsoon-like rains in May (usually the wettest month of the year in Texas) destroyed colonies around Corpus Christi. Many landlords pay close attention to weather forecasts and lower their houses a foot or two when high winds are predicted; however, they advise never to drop houses during the night as roosting birds may panic and never return.

Though most Purple Martins are killed by weather events, predators also take a toll. Martins are most vulnerable to predators when they are nestlings, but adults are also killed on the nests—especially by owls, which reach into the compartment to snag sleeping birds. Using one talon to hang onto a swinging gourd, owls have been seen to use the other talon to drag out occupants. Snakes swallow nestlings and adults in nest compartments, sometimes growing too swollen to leave the cavity. The Sharp-shinned Hawk, Cooper's Hawk, Merlin, Peregrine Falcon, and American Kestrel can be serious diurnal predators on adult martins in North America. These birds of prey make surprise attacks on a colony and capture adults and fledged young as they scatter.

Other predatory animals larger than a martin may prey upon birds; however, since martins are so swift and maneuverable, no predators specialize in hunting them. House cats are known to catch unwary birds when they land on the ground to eat grit or collect nest material. One observer was startled to see an adult Bald Eagle swoop down and grab a martin from a colony, while another witnessed a Great Blue Heron fly up and snap a passing martin. After catching a twelve-inch largemouth bass, a fisherman in Pennsylvania was surprised to find that the fish had consumed a Purple Martin—perhaps after it fell into the water or when it swooped to the lake surface for a drink.

Purple Martin Promotion

Over the past one hundred years, interest in and concern for the Purple Martins have expanded as individuals and communities have banded together to protect and manage nest colonies. There are at least ten regional and local associations and three national organizations dedicated to Purple Martins in North America. These are the Nature Society, which publishes *Nature Society News,* "the Voice of the Purple Martin," based in Griggsville, Illinois; the Purple Martin Conservation Association, located in Edinboro, Pennsylvania; and the Purple Martin Society, NA (North America), in Burr Ridge, Illinois.

The Nature Society, founded in 1962, proffers advice about feeding and housing native songbirds and wildlife and focuses on Purple Martin management in rural and suburban yards. The monthly thirty-or-so-page *Nature Society News* publishes tips about how to establish homes and control pesky sparrows and insect parasites. It lists bird arrivals and departures and publishes letters, poetry, and articles about Purple Martins and how to conserve them. Regular columnists also write about other bird favorites, such as hummingbirds, orioles, bluebirds, and the Whooping Crane.

Started by J. L. Wade, businessman and Griggsville resident, the Nature Society exemplified an entrepreneurial effort to attract both business and tourism to the small Illinois community by proclaiming Griggsville to be the martin capital of the nation. Wade began to manufacture aluminum nest houses for martins and actively promoted his firm's birdhouses throughout the United States and Canada. So-called Griggsville martin houses have popped up all over the U.S. South and Midwest and are featured in martin days and bird festivals. Over the years, Wade and his colleagues have modified the aluminum houses, adding accessories and customized systems. Currently, manufacturers offer owl guards, "dri-nest" subfloors, porch dividers, post sockets, and sparrow traps as additions to metal nest houses. Through *Nature Society News* and two books

FIGURE 11. Griggsville, Illinois. Photograph of Purple Martin Junction and promotion of martins as insect eaters. Photo courtesy of Nature Society, Purple Martin Junction, Griggsville, Illinois. Nature Society is the original Purple Martin organization, est. 1962.

he authored, Wade and Nature Society personnel have long alerted owners about usurper sparrows and starlings, plus predatory snakes and owls, as well as how to keep nests and nestlings relatively free of nest mites and blowflies.

The newspaper-sized publication prints five hundred or more letters per year, plus migration reports, and suggestions for nest house placement and colony management. The publication urges farmers, suburban Americans, and senior citizens to actively promote Purple Martin conservation by multiplying and sustaining successful colonies throughout the species' range. In recent years, discussion has focused on the growing deployment of painted or lacquered gourds and additional artificial piping as homes for martins.

A second national martin organization was founded by James R. Hill III. While studying martins, Hill grew concerned about the dependence of martins on humans for nest sites and in the gradual, long-term decline in overall populations documented by the North American Breeding Bird Survey. In 1987 Hill incorporated the Purple Martin Conservation Association (PMCA) in order to educate martin landlords on colony management practices. The association began to serve as a central data-gathering and information source about the species; it also funds research into martin biology.

The PMCA published the first volume of its newsletter, the *Purple Martin Update* (edited by Hill), in February 1988. This quarterly contains ten to fifteen articles about martin biology and colony management. To promote research and conservation, the PMCA has initiated three volunteer, citizen-science projects that collect martin nesting and migration data. A Colony Registration Program records the location of over fifty thousand Purple Martin nest sites across North America. In 1995 Project Martinwatch was established as a weekly nest-monitoring program. Landlords are encouraged to check their gourds or house compartments every five to seven days and to record the number and age of eggs or nestlings in each nest.

Beginning in 1998, the PMCA solicited volunteers to submit dates of arriving martins for its Scout Arrival Study. By mapping the thousands of reports submitted each year, the

PMCA has been able to improve the accuracy of maps depicting martin migration in North America.

As part of an effort to promote and improve the management of Purple Martin colonies, the PMCA began a landlord recognition program in 1992. Each year, the PMCA identifies a "Landlord of the Year" to recognize the achievements of individuals who have made innovative contributions to the welfare of the Purple Martin (see Table 6).

The PMCA has also recently started a Purple Martin Mentors Program, which encourages established martin landlords to help new recruits. Through e-mails and site visits, martin

TABLE 6. *PMCA Landlords of the Year*

Year	Name	Achievements
1992	Charles McEwan Moncton, N.B.	Designed starling-proof entrance holes and electrically heated martin houses. Video recorded the entire nesting season inside a martin compartment.
1993	Andrew Troyer Conneautville, Pa.	Implemented a new crank-up house design, removable nest inserts, access doors for natural gourds, sparrow and starling box traps, and a new martin capture technique.
1994	Terry Suchma Burr Ridge, Ill.	Created a Purple Martin Bulletin Board on Prodigy Internet service and conducted public education programs across the Midwest.
1995	Thomas Dellinger Duncanville, Tex.	Banded over 10,000 martins, pioneered nest compartment enlargement, mesh flooring for compartments, and injured martin rehabilitation.
1996	Ed Donath Arlington Heights, Ill.	Enlarged nesting compartments and experimented with supplemental feeding. Created new house designs and a system for aging martin nestlings.
1997	Chris Slabaugh Nappanee, Ind.	Published *Purple Martins: 400 Questions and Answers.* Made larger compartment house designs and slide-out nest trays.
1998	Kent Justus Little Rock, Ark.	Created the *Purple Martin Headquarters* and Purple Martin Forum on the World Wide Web.

mentors instruct new landlords in the art and science of martin landlording.

In 1993 the PMCA began to award small, annual research grants to students, professionals, and other individuals engaged in Purple Martin research. These $500 to $2,500 awards support the study of various aspects of martin conservation and biology, including efforts in establishing housing for Purple Martins in the Pacific Northwest, a study of differences in mitochondrial DNA between martin populations, NEXRAD mapping of martin roosts, and population studies in Baja California, Mexico.

As part of its mission to educate the public, the PMCA also supplies free information handouts, which can also be downloaded from its web site. Most of these handouts are aimed at helping new landlords. They include *Helpful Hints for Landlords, Attracting and Managing Purple Martins, Twelve Reasons Why People Lose Their Martins,* and *Top Ten Reasons Why People Fail to Attract Martins.* The PMCA also rents a program of seventy-five slide transparencies for public presentations.

The PMCA actively encourages its seven thousand or so members to modify martin houses for the birds' benefit. It suggests that landlords actively manage colonies by removing European Starlings and House Sparrows, installing starling-resistant entrance holes and predator guards on martin house poles. The PMCA also champions the use of natural and artificial gourds as martin housing. In 1991 it began promoting the use of a taped martin dawn song as a way to attract birds to new colonies, and in 1999 began marketing martin decoys as bird attractions. The PMCA operates the Martin Market Place, a source of approved houses, information, and housing accessories. These items can be ordered by mail or via a secure online service on their web site.

Both the Nature Society and the PMCA have been at the forefront of promoting interest and research into America's favorite bird, and they continue to encourage people with all levels of expertise and competency to guarantee a future for Purple Martins. Additional organizations with a strong interest in martin preservation are scattered across the breeding range of the Purple Martin in North America. Most of them are small, ranging in size from the Alamo Area Purple Martin Association with fewer than a dozen local members to the Purple Martin Society, North America, which has hundreds of affiliated landlords scattered across the nation.

The Alamo Area Purple Martin Association is a small local organization in south-central Texas that was organized on Texas Independence Day. Its members make public presentations, advise potential landlords, and mentor new enthusiasts in Seguin and New Braunfels, Texas. The American Bird Conservation Association based in Nappanee, Indiana, is dedicated to providing better housing and habitat for native cavity nesters, notably the Purple Martin and Eastern Bluebird. It provides members with information about how to attract martins and bluebirds, a colorful laminated decal of the association logo, and an annual report detailing the number of birds fledged through the efforts of association members.

In Canada the Association des Amateurs d'Hirondelles du Québec formed to unite the swallow enthusiasts and martin landlords of Quebec. The association seeks to support the nesting and expansion of martins in the province, and its effort to map martin colonies in Quebec has located nests in fifty-one cities. The association produces a biannual magazine, holds two meetings each year, and supports martin research. The group also hosts a twenty-foot-tall martin blind that was set up by Pierre Ducas in 1992 in the town of Chambly. In 1996 the association moved the tower to Valois Park along the edge of Lake St. Louis in Dorval. The blind is accessible through an interior staircase, from which viewers can peer inside Purple Martin nesting compartments. Recently, the association has sponsored the installation of additional towers hosting large martin colonies in Aylmer and St. Placide.

The Purple Martin Society of Collier County, organized in 1985, is based in southwest Florida. The society features field trips and provides members with a newsletter recapping the events of monthly meetings held in Collier County.

In 1999 a handful of landlords in Louisville started the Kentucky Purple Martin Association as a support group for martin landlords. The organization seeks to facilitate communication between the state's martin enthusiasts. A similar organization in the prairie provinces of Canada is the Manitoba Purple Martin Club based in Winnipeg. The Purple Martin and Bird Society of Southeastern New Brunswick was formed in 1968 and serves members in eastern Canada. Small Purple Martin organizations are springing up all over, including groups recently organized in north Texas and Wichita, Kansas.

The National Wildbird Refuge, Inc., is a unique martin organization. It is not a club for martin landlords. Based in Metairie, Louisiana, this organization began in 1983, when Carlyle Rogillio, a retired U.S. Air Force pilot and petroleum engineer, formed a Project Swallow Committee with local community members and business leaders interested in creating a sanctuary for Purple Martins that migrate through the New Orleans area. The project started as an injured martin rehabilitation effort at the Audubon Zoo, which resulted in the publication of Rogillio's *Purple Martin Rehabilitation Manual.*

At least one regional martin organization is expanding to attract martin landlords across North America. Terry Anne Suchma formed the Purple Martin Society, NA, in 1994 as an organization for landlords in Illinois. It now includes members from additional U.S. states and Canada, with the Purple Martin Society of Illinois forming a local chapter of the larger organization. Members receive *The Scout Report,* a newsletter produced three times each year, and gather for lunches, presentations, and workshops during spring and fall meetings in the Chicago area.

The Purple Martin Society web site provides a wealth of information about martin houses, accessories, and management. It also hosts an online discussion group—the RoundTable Conference. These two projects are geared to support the educational mission of this nonprofit organization dedicated to informing the public and potential landlords about Purple Martins.

In addition to specialized societies and organizations, over the years many local communities have capitalized on their relationship with Purple Martins. Perhaps the first community to celebrate the Purple Martin was Greencastle, Pennsylvania, which enjoys a bird tradition of "tameness" with the martins.

A visitor in the 1920s characterized the relationship as one of "friendly intimacy." Poles around the town square blossomed with plain, rectangular boxes used by nesting martins—"within easy reach of people passing by on the pavement." Nobody tampered with the boxes or the birds, which zoomed in and around the main street. Old-timers reckoned that Greencastle's love for martins dated to at least the 1840s. Fred Ziegler, who reported Greencastle's affection for the species, discovered that martins used boxes fixed on a tavern during the Civil War. Then, for some unknown reason, possibly related to the arrival of House Sparrows, a human generation passed before Purple Martins showed in town. Two older residents continued to supply boxes and helped the colony recover.

Every mid-March scouts arrive, and within a week or so, according to local lore, they guide additional migrants into the community. By mid-April most martin houses are filled with tenants, "and streets resound, of a morning, with cheery whistles," noted Ziegler. Nest building, feeding young, and harassing sparrows and cats filled the downtown with commotion. And then in August, migrants collected on wires and departed, "setting-out by night and generally going all at the same time," Ziegler recorded.

Greencastle's historic affection for Purple Martins is matched with experiences in Winona Lake, Indiana. Residents realized that the insect-hungry swallows feasted on unwanted bugs and set up houses that attracted more than eight hundred pairs in the decade after 1900. However, the most successful campaign to promote the Purple Martin and tend to its needs began over half a century later in the small Illinois town of Griggsville.

Momentum for promoting martin conservation grew after Rachel Carson's *Silent Spring* (1962) documented the side effects of chemical pesticides. J. L. Wade, whose company made TV and FM radio antennae, petitioned Griggsville Jaycees in the small community of 1,240 people to set up martin houses in order to eradicate biting mosquitoes and flies. Aluminum houses made by his company proved successful and drew media support. Within three years, some 120 martin houses lined streets and yards in the southwestern Illinois community, which capitalized on the success by proclaiming itself the "martin capital of the world."

With support from Griggsville citizens, Illinois's Governor Otto Kerner, and the mayors of Peoria and Rock Island, Wade and others began spring drives to interest people in these insectivorous birds. New support came from officials in Davenport and Waterloo, Iowa, and from as far away as Texarkana and Houston, Texas. Civic and service clubs in various communities began to promote martin houses as a means of raising concern for bird protection and funding local wildlife and other outdoor projects.

However, Griggsville was neither the first community to celebrate the Purple Martin (that honor goes to Greencastle, Pennsylvania), nor the only one to campaign for the martin, but "it was," as enthusiast Wade claimed, "the first to develop a sense of mission concerning the birds' welfare, and to push martins and all other wild birds into the national consciousness." In early years, Wade and promoter colleagues received assistance from two aluminum manufacturers; a hardware chain that boosted martin houses (selling more than 9,500 in a single month in 1966 to urban and rural fanciers); and a Chicago-based oil company. Martin Oil Company gave away houses and championed "Purple Martin ethyl" for auto maneuverability and quick starts. By the late 1960s, martin houses blossomed in parks, zoos (Marlin Perkins, Director of Forest Park Zoo in St. Louis and narrator of "Wild Kingdom," accepted a "castle" for his facility), preserves, motel parking lots, and race tracks in New York (Saratoga Springs), the Midwest, and the South—the bird's stronghold.

In April 1966, John K. Morris of Chadwick introduced House Bill 1058, which sought to switch Illinois's state bird from the Northern Cardinal to the Purple Martin. Sponsors argued that martins combined beauty and utility (financial advantages of locating the martin's "capital" in Illinois didn't escape them) with novelty. Residents needed a boost from this energetic and useful martin, rather than stick with a pretty bird that six additional states had also adopted.

Defenders of the cardinal reminded citizens that in 1929, schoolchildren had preferred the redbird over the Eastern Bluebird and three other species (none of them the martin) to be chosen Illinois's official bird. Illinois was the second state (after Kentucky) to stake its claim to the cardinal—an esteemed resident; the Purple Martin passed only the summer in Illinois. Some opposed the switch from the cardinal to the martin "because of the proposal's commercial aspects" (referring to Griggsville-type houses made by Wade's firm) and criticized Purple Martins for depending on human largesse. As controversy mounted, Representative Morris withdrew his bill.

Other communities, according to Wade, followed Griggsville's lead. Residents in LaVerne, Iowa, put up fourteen boxes in the mid-1960s and enjoyed fewer pesky insects, as did people in Walnut Ridge, Arkansas. Birds flocked to some five hundred martin houses in that community of 3,500 (in 1966) and reportedly feasted on biting insects. Parsons, Kansas, has recently proclaimed itself the Martin Capital of Kansas and has organized an annual festival for martin enthusiasts. Additional communities noted for martin promotion include Lake Charles, Louisiana; Fort Smith, Arkansas; Huntsville, Alabama; Bruce, Mississippi; Bass Lake, Indiana; Lennox, South Dakota; Trenton, New Jersey; and Moncton, New Brunswick. Currently, the towns of Dorval, LaSalle, and Rosemere vie for the title of martin capital of Quebec.

In 1991 Harold Coates, the owner of a martin house manufacturing company in Bossier City, Louisiana, proposed to construct a suite of martin boxes as a fitting memorial to the military who had fought in Operation Desert Storm. With funding from a military officers' association at nearby Barksdale Air Force Base, Coates set up an array of martin boxes, including one eighty-six-compartment behemoth, surrounded by a brick column fence and walkway. The park was dedicated as a Living Memorial on 4 July 1991 and is billed by Bossier City as the world's first and only memorial to the Gulf War troops.

Previously, the Young Men's Business Club of Lake Charles, Louisiana, had dedicated a 120-foot candelabra with forty-six hexagonal martin houses and 2,640 nesting compartments as a Living Memorial to the servicemen who died and served in Vietnam (see Figure 12). This tall tower, erected in 1980, sits on the shores of Lake Charles. According to local enthusiasts, it forms the handle of "a mosquito-hungry umbrella of martins . . . hovering over the city."

With the rapid expansion of the Internet during the 1990s, new communities promoted the Purple Martin online. As Internet service providers began attracting customers, Terry Suchma set up electronic martin bulletin boards with AOL and Prodigy Internet services, creating an online forum for discussion of martin conservation and landlording. She has recently consolidated these electronic discussion groups as part of the RoundTable Conference set up through the Purple Martin Society web site.

In January 1998, Kent Justus of Little Rock, Arkansas, established another popular online discussion group when he formed the Purple Martin Forum. Now hosted by the Purple Martin Conservation Association, this discussion group allows posts and queries on a World Wide Web site. Discussions range from how to attract martins, care of nestlings, nest site competitors, and predator eradication. As with all online communities, frequent contributors become semilegendary; expert landlords and expressive individuals provide entertainment and information for hundreds of martin enthusiasts who regularly surf the site.

Many members of the Purple Martin Forum also subscribe to the Purplemartin e-mail list, which gives subscribers another way to communicate and discuss their favorites. Founded in February 2000, the Purplemartin list quickly attracted over one hundred subscribers posting hundreds of messages every month.

As martin landlords discuss their birds online, they create a Purple Martin subculture, with accepted rules of discourse and associated jargon. There are frequent references to scumbeaks and sparrownasties (European Starlings and House Sparrows—also referred to as S&S), SREHs (starling-resistant entrance holes), and DE (diatomaceous earth—a whitish substance made up of tiny silica shells from freshwater colonial algae—that is spooned under the nests or subfloors of chambers in order to control nest mites). The coarse silica crystals scour the exoskeletons of parasitic mites and insects, leading to their desic-

FIGURE 12. Community-sponsored towers and roosts have attracted public support. This one in Lake Charles, Louisiana, is a Vietnam War Memorial. Courtesy Gay Gomez.

cation and death. Some martin groups recommend it. Others claim that the tablespoon of DE gets blown about in the cavity and inhaled. A "no chemical" approach favors nest replacements and wood shavings as ways of controlling nest parasites.

Martin house manufacturers have also created a web presence, and potential martin landlords can order a variety of houses, gourds, and other products online. Many dedicated individuals have created their own Purple Martin web sites, which often provide the latest opinions or insider perspectives on managing a martin colony. Chuck Abare, an engineer in northern Alabama, created one site that has become popular with martin enthusiasts. *Chuck's Purple Martin Page* features pictures of the gourd rack he designed, information about landlording innovations, and links to additional martin web sites. His web page also provides a martin "Chatterbox"—listing hundreds of martin landlords, complete with contact information and a brief description of their martin colony—that serves as an additional index for martin enthusiasts to identify one another and share information. Kent Justus and Steve Kroenke established a *Purple Martin Headquarters* on the World Wide Web, which provides information from published sources as well as credible observations about their own Purple Martin colonies.

There are now enough web pages to support a Purple Martin Web Ring that links over a dozen affiliated sites, and any major search engine quickly reveals additional sites about martin life history and management. As web sites proliferate, the online martin community provides the means to unite interested enthusiasts.

This online martin community resulted in a get-together of martineers. In 1998 Kent Justus and a small group of martin landlords, who had corresponded through the Purple Martin Forum, agreed to meet on the Finger, Tennessee, farm belonging to Victor Stoll. The Stoll Family Farm, purported to be the largest martin breeding colony (of four hundred pairs) in North America, also hosted "MartinFest '99." It drew over one hundred landlords from across the country, and MartinFest is now an annual event.

Landlords

*R*oger Tory Peterson, the late field guide author, artist, and dean of American bird-watchers, didn't like the label "bird lover." "I don't love birds," he said, "I am obsessed with birds. I have always been obsessed with birds. But I don't love them. Loving demands reciprocation, or at least the promise of reciprocation. Birds simply do not reciprocate. We might enjoy them, watch them, and study them, but to 'love' them—that is being too anthropomorphic."

Many people who provide housing for Purple Martins disagree with Peterson's statement, claiming to love birds, at least those birds they spend so much time with during spring and summer. Though wild birds may not have reciprocated Peterson's interest in them, it is not uncommon for landlords to state that Purple Martins reward their attention. These people are realistic about martins and do not make fanciful claims, but experience tells them that the martins show a measure of responsiveness to and confidence in human efforts on their behalf. This chapter celebrates a reciprocal relationship between humans and birds. Purple Martins confide their wildness to us by permitting, indeed some claim welcoming, our close approach. Through their temperament and characteristics of territorial display and defense, martins demonstrate qualities that we admire. Migratory flights amaze us, as do their abilities to adjust to our activities in and around rural and suburban areas. Though human-introduced bird competitors have dealt a blow to martin survival, the species responds well to colony management.

Sailing high over suburban and rural yards, Purple Martins continue a relationship with humans that spans at least hundreds of years. By most accounts, the birds benefit from this association as much as humans do. Martins receive a safe place to nest and raise young, while humans gain satisfaction from admiring and helping such lively and beneficial birds. The relationship connects people, who choose to place a martin house on their property, with wild birds that freely select sites set out for them.

Bottle or birdhouse gourds (*Lagenaria siceraria*) were the original martin compartments set out by Native Americans. Though a tradition of providing gourds for martins to nest in continued in southern states, sentiment shifted toward constructing wooden martin houses or boxes—often designed to look like miniature human dwellings. Until the 1960s, martin landlords built martin houses ranging from simple wood boxes with entrance holes, to fanciful designs crafted to suit individual tastes. Then, commercially made metal houses proved effective nest sites.

In 1905 *Bird-Lore* published an article with instructions for building martin homes, complete with illustrations of finished domiciles. Author J. Warren Jacobs supplied instructions that are the lasting basis for success: nest boxes must have pitched roofs, be painted white, stand on a pole twelve to fifteen feet from the ground, and be positioned twenty or more feet from buildings or tree branches that may interfere with flight lines of entry and exit. Jacobs made a line of elegant miniature Victorian houses, some of which Canadian conservationist Jack Miner purchased in 1913. As the proprietor of the Jacobs Birdhouse Company in Waynesburg, Pennsylvania, until his death in 1947, Jacobs preferred to craft abodes that resemble human dwellings for his martins, rather than plainer bird boxes. His penchant for making homes fit for "little people," such as Purple Martins, blended sentiment with utility in the move to protect wild birds in the early 1900s. Jacobs is most famous for a line of "Capital" martin houses that feature up to 104 rooms, weigh over eight hundred pounds apiece, and tower over six-feet tall. Creations featured columns, a capital dome, and a tower clock with its face always painted to mark 8:25, the exact time of the end of the Spanish American War. Capital martin houses were expensive, costing $185 in 1928.

Enormous martin dwellings made by Jacobs could attract "super colonies." In 1909 New York state farmer C. E. Hamilton claimed three hundred useful martins nested in two large houses and supplied details about spring arrival—"they all come at once," he noted—in what the journal's editors reported was one of the largest colonies in the nation.

FIGURE 13. (*a*) J. Warren Jacobs, of Waynesburg, Pennsylvania, instructed Audubon Society readers in 1905 about constructing martin houses. (*b*) Martin House No. 2 has thirty-six rooms, with tobacco crates added as wooden cylinders. (From *Bird-Lore*, 1905)

FIGURE 14. Junior Audubon members paid ten cents for a button and leaflets and joined in school classes to construct houses for wild birds. This group from the Riverside, Tennessee, Junior Audubon Class was among ten thousand children enrolled during the school year in fifteen southern states in 1912. (From *Bird-Lore*).

Though wooden martin "houses" continue to be popular with hobbyists, in recent decades many commercially available martin houses have been constructed out of aluminum after J. L. Wade pioneered his units in 1962. Wade also started a tradition of giving house designs letter and number designations—his first design is labeled the M-12K, which is short for Musselman 12 compartment, since it features a twelve-compartment, two-story design built to specifications originally provided by naturalist and friend T. E. Musselman.

Subsequent designs marketed by Wade included his Trio line: the TG-8 (eight-compartment Trio Grandma), TG-12 (twelve-compartment Trio Grandpa), TW-12 (Trio Wade twelve-compartment house), and the TM-12 (twelve-compartment hexagonal Trio Minicastle). The largest aluminum house built by Nature House, Inc., and marketed by the Nature Society, is the PMC-24, a hexagonal Purple Martin Castle with twenty-four compartments. The same firm also manufactures three less expensive twelve-compartment martin houses advertised as its Duracraft line. Compartments in each of these houses measure six-by-six-by-six inches, which has proven acceptable to martins and much less acceptable to competitor starlings.

Several companies followed Wade's lead and began marketing aluminum martin houses. By 1990 the five leading manufacturers of martin housing (Heath, Nature House, Inc., Coates, Mac Industries, and Birds Limited, Inc.) had combined sales of over 125,000 units, which total about $25 million per year. Landlords find aluminum houses attractive because they are relatively inexpensive and easy to take care of, though some enthusiasts prefer to make their own structures out of wood.

People who build their own martin houses are weekend wood- and metal-workers and also observers interested in upgrading houses. Andrew Troyer, an Amish martin landlord from Pennsylvania, designed a fourteen-compartment house (T-14) to incorporate the latest martin research. He included larger compartments six-by-six-by-twelve inches that appear to improve nest success. Landlords without the requisite woodworking skills, yet wanting houses with larger compartments, may contact Lone Star Martin Houses based in McQueeney, Texas.

This commercial outlet offers several models constructed from durable aluminum with variously shaped entrances that keep European Starlings out and with balconies that single aggressive male martins find harder to defend.

For landlords interested in low-cost, effective martin housing, the PMCA has championed the traditional use of gourds. Landlords may grow the gourds themselves or purchase them from a number of suppliers. After they are hollowed out, treated with a preservative, and painted white, these gourds are hung individually or clustered on a rack. Though some manufacturers argue against the use of martin gourds, many landlords believe them safe, effective, and popular among birds when used according to guidelines.

Plastic gourds are now being marketed to counter claims that natural gourds are unsafe and hard to maintain. Artificial gourds are manufactured by several companies, including an eight-inch diameter version produced by Carroll Industries. Some landlords complain that, as they are made of two halves that must be taken apart for cleaning or nest checking, they may need to be sealed with an epoxy for weatherproofing. However, the eleven-inch diameter Natureline Gourds manufactured by Plasticraft, and ten-inch diameter SuperGourds marketed by the PMCA, feature access parts for easy nest monitoring and cleaning. In many areas, martins have taken well to the natural and artificial gourds, with many landlords reporting high occupancy rates when compartments are suspended from racks. In 2001 Andrew Troyer, through his Birds' Paradise business, began to market the new Troyer Horizontal Gourd. These white plastic gourds are hung horizontally, with the entrance hole located at the end of the long gourd neck, making the nest compartment a predator-resistant fourteen inches beyond the opening.

In addition to assessing the number and types of nest facilities, martin landlords face even more choices about colony management. These range from simple placement of a house or gourd on a pole, to daily maintenance through nest inspections and removal of sparrows or starlings. For some, it may mean letting nature take its course because those people have little time to monitor or attend to the needs of nesting birds.

However, landlords who wish to invest time in a martin colony have a variety of management techniques at their disposal. Purple Martins have drawn a cohort of mechanically minded folks, who are dedicated to innovative practices. Wade's adoption of aluminum houses has evolved over the past forty years to debates about compartment size, positioning, and access.

Recent trends include larger nesting compartments (to reduce predation and chick crowding), starling-resistant entrance holes (SREHs, which are oval, crescent, or half-moon shapes that the more robustly built alien birds find hard to squeeze through), and nest replacements (artificial nests to replace ones infested by mites or other parasites). Darwin "Dean" Mosman of Iowa was among the first to experiment with larger nesting compartments. Mosman and colleagues discovered that martins will lay more eggs and fledge more young in compartments larger than the six-by-six-inch format used by commercial manufacturers. Building houses with larger compartments, or removing interior walls of older ones, adds extra space and safety from owls, crows, jays, and other predators that reach in and snag birds.

However, landlords quickly discovered that European Starlings, previously rare occupants of the smaller nest compartments, relish these more spacious units. Landlords have experimented with half-moon or crescent entrance shapes to exclude these aliens. Martins, with their short legs, pass through odd-shaped holes, whereas longer-shanked starlings find it harder to navigate them. Terry Suchma suggests that crescent-shaped SREHs are most successful, and another excluder (a bat-winged design) also shows promise. She notes, however, that round, natural-appearing entrance holes give martins easiest access, and warns that landlords should permit their charges to nest successfully on a site at least once before switching to SREHs. There is a good chance, she argues, that martins will reject houses fitted solely with starling excluders and search elsewhere for nest sites. Several landlords have turned the crescent-shaped SREHs upside down to make them easier for martins to enter, and they debate the merits of additional SREH shapes on various PM forums.

Nest replacement is another novel practice. Organizations such as the PMCA and the Purple Martin Society, NA, recommend replacing wet or parasite-ridden nests with artificial heavy-duty polystyrene or natural products. In order to facilitate nest replacement, some landlords, especially those in Amish country, place removable nest inserts in cavities. These are wooden insert trays with a nest cup carved into the rear, which can be lined with replaceable wood shavings that martins seem to accept. The Purple Martin Society, NA, does not recommend aromatic cedar chips, as they may compromise the lungs of nestlings.

For years, landlords have noticed that one or two older male martins may dominate nest cavities adjacent to the compartment they select and keep other birds away. By placing wooden dividers on the porches, Carlyle Rogillio of Metairie, Louisiana, was able to keep males from defending the neighboring compartments. Reduction of this so-called Male Porch Dominance increased occupancy and fledging rates on his Louisiana site, and the PMCA, Purple Martin Society, NA, and other organizations recommend that landlords add porch dividers to their houses. Dividers also prevent nestlings from wandering into nearby cavities and mingling with different-aged young. Some birds fall off porches, become "lost," or when outside, make easy targets for passing hawks.

Terrestrial predators, such as snakes and raccoons, climb poles to take birds and eggs. Various predator guards, usually conical or tubular barriers or skirts, around poles may prevent animals from reaching the nest compartments. However, a few landlords have adopted electrical controls. When snakes were found entering bluebird boxes in South Carolina, for instance, local farmers began electrifying a metal strip below their bird houses, which shocked any snake or other climber. Martin landlords Rocky Goforth of Smyrna, South Carolina, and Gary Tessneer of Shelby, North Carolina, place a strip of electrified copper or other suitable tubing up the poles of their martin colony.

In order to keep owls from raiding martin houses, many landlords place wire cages around houses. Walt Lutz of Oklahoma deserves credit for "flipper bars" that he positioned about a martin-length (seven inches) in front of the entrance hole. These baffles prevent predatory birds from reaching inside the cavity. Recent designs include similar wires to keep owls away from gourd entrances.

Additionally, many older martins reach colonies before the threat of cold weather has passed. Some landlords in the Midwest heat houses for early arrivals, and even include heated roost boxes (pioneered by Robert Ring of Wisconsin) in which martins may shelter during freezing temperatures and snow flurries. Within the last decade or so, a few innovative landlords claim to have trained martins to take food, such as mealworms and crickets, during bad weather. A *Purple Martin Update* account (9[4]: 26–28) by Ken Kostka explains how he and Amish landlord Andy Troyer set out to save weather-affected birds in April 2000. Kostka purchased crickets and, together with Troyer and Troyer's son, began tossing them in the air close to famished martins. One bird, then another, responded by swooping from perches and catching crickets in midair. Kostka judged that as many as forty martins fed on seven hundred live, six-week-old crickets on that late April day. He expressed confidence that such a feeding strategy (including setting out insects on house porches) can sustain birds for about three consecutive days when flying insects are scarce or absent. This happens when there is a combination of constant daylight temperatures at 50–45 degrees F or lower, steady rain, high winds, and fog.

In 1991, after research indicated that yearling martins (birds likely to colonize a new site) are attracted by early morning songs, the PMCA began to market a tape of the species dawn song. The tape featured 60 minutes of dawn song recorded by Eugene S. Morton at his colony in Severna Park, Maryland. In 1997, after the tape had proven successful, the PMCA also issued a recording on compact disk. Currently, there are two lure-type tapes that broadcast usual martin "chatter" in a colony. The Purple Martin Society recommends that the "Ultimate Purple Martin Lure" (71 minutes of uninterrupted purple martin sounds) be played during the final six weeks of the nest season, when adults and fledged young roam about prospecting for future nest sites.

Additional devices consist of carved martin decoys designed by Pennsylvania landlord Lester Keck, who published plans for them. When placed on or around houses, the painted look-alikes are intended to attract passing birds. The first batch offered by the PMCA in 2000 quickly sold out.

New houses and innovations intended to improve occupancy rates and nesting success appeal to mechanically inclined landlords—a small, but growing, cadre of enthusiasts. Many other bird lovers check martin nests every five to seven days, ensuring as far as possible that the nestlings fledge successfully. Many landlords claim that such practices are important, but not the most essential for colony management.

The most important duty, they say, is to deter and eliminate House Sparrows and European Starlings. Experts argue that no one should put up a martin house without being prepared to battle these exotic species. New landlords finding their way to the Purple Martin Forums or other Internet sites quickly learn that pest control is crucial for being a successful landlord. The PMCA, Purple Martin Society, NA, and martin house manufacturers, such as the Nature Society, sell sparrow traps (as there are no entrance sizes or shapes that will deter sparrows but permit martins), and discussion of starling eradication is frequent fare on the web sites. Forum advocates of pest control chide martin lovers who are too squeamish to trap or shoot alien avians. When Rob Fergus reported that a starling fed a nestling martin in Austin, Texas, the event sparked additional rounds of anti-starling posts.

When polled about their greatest trials and frustrations in caring for martins, the majority of nearly one hundred respondents stated that pest management was a constant problem. Landlords expressed sadness about losses from predators, inclement weather, and nest mishaps. However, in this unofficial survey, most martin managers suggested that the pleasures of landlording far outweighed the trials and that one of the hardest things about being a landlord was how much they missed the birds after the summer season (some term it "PM depression").

FIGURE 15. Landlords monitor birds in backyard aluminum houses and gourds and alter the shape and position of the entrances to exclude interloper starlings. These houses are from Seguin, Texas. Courtesy Robin Doughty.

The joy derived from observing and recording Purple Martin antics is a primary inducement for becoming a martin landlord. Many colony managers start out the day by checking their birds, and prefer to be around as their charges settle in for the night. For these martineers, bird colonies, like aquaria, relieve the routine and stresses of commuter lifestyles, by adding color and a focus to their lives. However, unlike aquarium fish, martins are free to come and go. Many landlords admire this freedom and are touched that such free-flying birds decide to nest in human-made cavities. They take pride in observing and figuring out the lives of these wild birds, reckoning that a growth in numbers repays their kindness.

East of the Rocky Mountains, the Purple Martin is now mostly dependent on nest compartments supplied by humans (although one or more pairs have successfully nested in old woodpecker cavities in dead cabbage palms [*Sabal palmetto*] in the Orlando Wetlands Park—a constructed wastewater treatment site in Florida—since 1993). Martin landlords know this and see themselves as both guardians and friends of the birds. With about 6 million martins living in more than a million colonies throughout North America, no individual can claim to have an impact on the population. But many thousands of enthusiasts, who take pride in supplying nest sites and making conditions for breeding optimal, perform a critical service. They enhance production, stabilize colony size, and instruct others about management techniques when martin numbers appear to be fluctuating, especially on the north edge of the bird's nesting range. The future of the Purple Martin is tied to the cumulative generosity of thousands of human landlords.

FIGURE 16. Male Purple Martin.
Courtesy John L. Tveten.

FIGURE 17. Female Purple Martin.
Courtesy John L. Tveten.

FIGURE 18. Female Purple Martin, feeding its young.
Courtesy John L. Tveten.

Further Reading and Resources

Three books deal directly with the Purple Martin. Two of them, written by expert and promoter J. L. Wade, reflect his interest in providing nest houses and in promoting his home base in Griggsville, Illinois, as the Purple Martin capital of the nation. His most recent book is *Attracting Purple Martins* (Griggsville, Illinois: Nature Society, 1987), in which Wade also observed martins and gathered valuable information about the biology of the species from correspondence and articles that have appeared in publications of *Nature Society News,* published by the Nature Society, the original Purple Martin organization, founded in 1962 and based in that Illinois community. More recently, Donald and Lillian Stokes and Justin L. Brown have compiled the *Stokes Purple Martin Book* (Boston: Little, Brown and Co., 1997), an important do-it-yourself treatment for potential martin landlords. The slim volume gives instructions for houses and colony management.

There are hundreds of published articles, essays, and news accounts about Purple Martins. Research papers appear in ornithological journals, such as the *Auk, Wilson Bulletin,* and *Condor,* plus other biological publications, and amply reward those who wish to puzzle over the ecology and behavior of the bird. Banding studies, nest monitoring, and migration figure prominently in such periodicals. The most recent review of this literature is the comprehensive life history account written by Charles R. Brown for *The Birds of North America* series, no. 287 (Philadelphia: Academy of Natural Sciences, and Washington, D.C.: American Ornithologist's Union, 1997).

We mention many important and interesting martin articles and studies in the text. P. A. Taverner and R. H. Swales, "The Birds of Point Pelee," *Wilson Bulletin* 20 (1908): 79–96, explore diurnal migration and fall weather. P. A. Taverner, "A Purple Martin Roost," *Wilson Bulletin* 18 (1906): 87–92, provides a lively account of an urban roost (in Chicago). The report on banded martins recovered in Central and South America is discussed in James R. Hill and Thomas B. Dellinger, "Purple Martin Recoveries South of the Border," *Purple Martin Update* 8(1) (December 1997): 28–29. Ken Kostka describes his latest attempts to help martins make it through cold weather in "Cricket Tossing: A New Emergency Feeding Technique for Purple Martins," *Purple Martin Update* 9(4) (September 2000): 26–28.

The José Antonio Alzate Ramírez article "Las golondrinas" (in Spanish) is found in the *Antología Universal Ilustrada* (London and Buenos Aires: Sociedad Internacional, no date), 25:12458–12464, while an accessible summary and discussion was published by María Dellinger in "The Swallows of Father Alzate," *Scout Report* 6(3) (Fall 1999): 26, 29–30.

Aldo Leopold's early note on his martin box in New Mexico is found in his article "Do Purple Martins Inhabit Bird Boxes in the West?" *Condor* 20 (May 1918): 93. One of the earliest U.S. discussions of the martin is found in Alan Feduccia, ed., *Catesby's Birds of Colonial America* (Chapel Hill, University of North Carolina Press, 1985), 94–95. Alexander Wilson's discussion of Purple Martins is found in T. M. Brewer, *Wilson's American Ornithology* (Boston: Otis, Broaders, 1840), 365–369.

Historically significant scientific studies noted in the section on life history studies include Jerome Jackson and J. Tate's "An Analysis of Nest Box Use by Purple Martins, House Sparrows, and Starlings in Eastern North America," *Wilson Bulletin* 86 (1974): 435–449. S. Rowher and D. M. Niles published their ground-breaking "An Historical Analysis of Spring Arrival Times in Purple Martins: A Test of Two Hypotheses" in *Bird Banding* 48 (1977): 162–167. Among the many significant contributions of Eugene S. Morton, a standout is the article he co-authored with K. C. Derrickson, "The Biological Significance of Age-Specific Return Schedules in Breeding Purple Martins," *Condor* 92 (1990): 1040–1050.

The DNA study exploring the evolutionary relationships and ancestry of martins is published in F. H. Sheldon and D. W. Winkler, "Intergeneric Phylogenetic Relationships of Swallows Estimated by DNA-DNA Hybridization," *Auk* 110 (1993): 798–824. In 1996 Kevin R. Russell and Sidney A. Gauthreaux began publishing their radar studies of martin roosts in "Monitoring Purple Martin Roosts with Weather Radar," *Purple Martin Update* 7(1) (1996): 2–6. See also Kevin Russell, David S. Mizrahi, and Sydney Gauthreaux, "Large-scale Mapping of Purple Martin Pre-Migratory Roosts," *Journal of Field Ornithology* 69(2) (Spring 1998): 316–325.

The history of Carlyle Rogillio's work in Louisiana was most recently reported in the November 2000 *Nature Society News.* The Punta Allen, Yucatan, martin roost is described by Krista Morgan in the September 1999 *Nature Society News.* Martins wintering in North America are discussed on page 17 of the October 1999 *Nature Society News.* Victor Stoll documents double-brooding in martins in his article "Do Purple Martins Ever Raise Two Broods?" *Nature Society News,* October 1999, 18.

The classic article on martin vocalizations is Charles R. Brown, "Vocalizations of the Purple Martin," *Condor* 86 (1984): 433–442. The martin dawn song is described in Eugene S. Morton, "Dawnsong of the Purple Martin," *Atlantic Naturalist* 38 (1988): 38–48.

The quotation from Roger Tory Peterson is found in his authorized biography, John C. Devlin and Grace Naismith, *The World of Roger Tory Peterson* (New York: Times Books, 1977).

Articles on martin colony management techniques appear in each quarterly edition of the *Purple Martin Update,* published by the Purple Martin Conservation Association. An interesting history of artificial martin gourds is reviewed in James R. Hill III, "The Evolution of the Plastic Purple Martin Gourd," *Purple Martin Update* 7(4) (September 1997): 26–27. Carlyle Rogillio's *Purple Martin Rehabilitation Manual* was published by the Nature Society in 1998. The November 2000 *Nature Society News* gives information on the treatment of martin nests with diatomaceous earth, while Purple Martins nesting in natural palms in Florida are described by Mark Sees in "Natural Nesting of Purple Martins," *Scout Report* 6(1) (June 1999): 31.

Associations established for the promotion of martins play an important role in both publicizing and protecting martins. Mention has already been made of the Nature Society, the Purple Martin Conservation Association, and the Purple Martin Society, NA, which actively work to bolster numbers throughout North America. Chat lines and web sites are a new and increasingly commonly used link in disseminating information, answering questions, sharing experiences, and updating information about martin behavior, distribution, and numbers. We have been especially impressed with the scope of coverage given to the bird by people of various backgrounds, ages, and diverse geographic areas. The following web sites are useful ways to ease oneself into the culture of martin lore:

Purple Martin Forum
(http://forum.purplemartin.org/forum)

Purple Martin Conservation Association
(www.purplemartin.org)

Purple Martin Society Webpage
(www.purplemartins.com)

Chuck's Purple Martin Page
(http://home.HiWAAY.net/~yankee1/)

Purple Martin House
(www.sound.net/~deadbird)

Purple Martin Headquarters
(www3.vantek.net/pmh)

Danny's Purple Martin Place
(www.brightok.net/~dfrazier)

The Nature Society
(www.naturesociety.org)

Purple Martin Webring
(http://www.webring.org/cgi-bin/
webring?ring=purplemartin;id=3;list)